PRAISE FOR VIVIEN'S RAIN

"Facing a child's illness is perhaps a parent's most daunting task. *Vivien's Rain* is one family's poignant story of dealing with epilepsy, the health care system, and their own broken dreams. A compelling and helpful read."

—Pete Earley, bestselling author of *Crazy: A Father's Search Through America's Mental Health Madness* and *Hot House: Life Inside Leavenworth Prison*

"*Vivien's Rain* is an inspirational journey into the heart of one family's struggle with epilepsy."

—Danielle Bacher, *LA Weekly*, *Rolling Stone* and *Playboy*

"*Vivien's Rain* is a very clear road map down the path of epilepsy. It is enlightening, harrowing, and heartening in equal measure."

—Beverly Archer, actress, *Major Dad* and *Mama's Family*

Vivien's Rain

My Daughter's Battle with Epilepsy

For
MEGAN and J.T.
Keep Fighting!

Mike Knox

Cover designed by: Siori Kitajima, SFAppWorks LLC
www.sfappworks.com
Cover illustration by Siori Kitajima
Formatting by Siori Kitajima and Ovidiu Vlad,
SFAppWorks LLC
E-book Formatted by Ovidiu Vlad

Cataloging-in-Publication data for this book is available from the Library of Congress

ISBN-13: 978-0-9895241-9-3
ISBN-10: 0989524191

Published by The Sager Group LLC
www.TheSagerGroup.Net
info@TheSagerGroup.Net

Vivien's Rain

*My Daughter's
Battle with Epilepsy*

BY MIKE KNOX

THE SAGER GROUP

Artifex Te Adiuva

FOR VIVIEN

*Do not pray for an easy life,
pray for the strength to endure a difficult one.*
—Bruce Lee

Contents

Chapter One
THE SEIZURE

I woke up to my wife, Nicole, screaming my name in anguish. As I opened my eyes, she rushed into the room. Our twenty-three-month-old daughter Vivien was limp in her arms, foaming at the mouth.

"She won't wake up!"

Nicole ran into our bathroom and splashed water on Vivien's face. I was still half asleep. It felt like I was still dreaming. I checked Vivien's pulse. It was faint. She was breathing, but she was out cold. I was astonished by how limp her body was. She only weighed twenty-six pounds, but she felt like lead.

I stuck my finger into her mouth to make sure she wasn't choking on a toy. I pried her eyes open and let go. The eyelids fluttered and closed. I dialed 911. It was busy.

"Hospital!" I yelled. I grabbed my jeans and shoes, dressing on the way out the door.

We ran into the cold morning. It was December, a day before Vivien's second birthday. Nicole had planned to take her to the zoo. Limp as she was, we tried to put her in the car seat then realized it was probably better to hold her and make sure she kept breathing. Nicole took her usual seat, front passenger. I put Vivien in her lap.

Pulling out of the driveway, I struggled to plot my route. We hadn't been to the hospital in two years. I wasn't even sure I remembered where it was.

"There's an urgent care down the street," Nicole said.

I drove east. The urgent care clinic was located in a strip mall, but it didn't open until eight a.m. Henry Mayo Hospital was five miles away. With the lights and rush-hour traffic, I knew it would take us at least twenty minutes to get there.

I headed south, down Seco Canyon Road. Parents were dropping off their children at Santa Clarita Elementary School. Traffic was stopped. Like a maniac, I drove down the median. Cars honked. I jumped a curb and took the sidewalk to cut across to another street, barely missing a crossing guard. I dialed 911 again. Still busy. My mouth was dry. I was running on pure fear. These are the moments in your life when everything comes crashing down. You think: *If only I could have been better prepared. If only I could have been a better father, a better husband.* You think of all the things you'd do differently if you could only change this one moment in time.

We had put Vivien to bed the night before with no problems. She even wanted us to kiss her Barbie dolls good night. *What if I never get to say good night to her again?*

Nicole's skin was pale and her eyes were distant. I'd had plenty of first aid and emergency medical training during my career; I wondered if she was going into shock. She was a mother in fear of losing her child, clinging to her baby. I wanted to tell her everything was going to be okay, but I could barely speak. My voice was harsh.

"Sing to her."

"What?'

"Sing something so that she knows we're here. Maybe she can hear us. Sing *Little Einsteins!*"

It was Vivien's favorite cartoon show, about four kids who go on adventures in a red rocket ship. Nicole sang, but it wasn't her voice. It was cracked and raw. Her lips trembled. She was petrified.

Nicole continued to sing. The morning traffic became increasingly heavy.

When we reached the Henry Mayo Hospital, I couldn't find the emergency entrance. I felt foolish for not knowing. I should have had a plan. I should have prepared for this. Every kid gets sick. Every kid needs to go to the emergency room at some point. Why hadn't I thought this through? *What kind of father am I?*

"It's in the back," Nicole said. She knew. She *always* knew. Thank God for her, again.

I drove to the back of the hospital. EMERGENCY ENTRANCE. Jumped out of the Jeep, left it running at the curb, and ran with Nicole to the entrance. Some firemen were walking out through the heavy sliding glass doors. "Help us!" I pleaded. "She's dying!"

One of the guys looked our way. He had blond hair and a baby face. He seemed bored. "She's just having a seizure," he said matter-of-factly.

Just a seizure?

As we passed the threshold of Emergency, Nicole screamed out in alarmed anguish, "Please help us!" The sound was blood-chilling; I'd never heard anything like it.

The events flowed. I felt one time removed, like a ghost watching from another dimension. A nurse led us to a small room. Nicole placed Vivien on a gurney. More nurses rushed in. They ran an IV and placed an oxygen mask over her face. They cut off her teddy bear pajamas and taped electrode sensors onto her chest.

Finally the doctor entered the room. He was an older man with a kind face but he looked exhausted. Like someone coming off a twelve-hour shift.

"What happened?" he asked calmly.

"We picked her up from her crib and brought her here. She won't wake up."

"I think she's having a seizure. Does she have a history of seizures?"

I looked at him blankly.

He administered a dose of Ativan. The seconds ticked by. The drug didn't work, so he gave her a second dose. Then a third. Nothing. She was still unconscious.

"She's about to go into cardiac arrest. Her vitals are bad," the doctor said. "I think her airways might be constricted. She's going to suffocate if she doesn't get more oxygen. I might have to cut open her trachea."

Just then, a Catholic priest came into the room and before we knew it he was administering last rites. *Noooooo.*

Everything was happening so fast. *What the hell? She does not need last rites. SHE IS NOT NEAR DEATH. Who called this silly guy in the penguin suit? He must be in the wrong room."*

At last, words came to my tongue. "Why are you here?" I demanded.

"To help your child be with God."

"I don't want her to be with God. I want her to be with *me*. Here on Earth, where she belongs."

Her pulse faded. Machines beeped rapidly.

"I will pray for her," the priest said.

"Get the defibrillator," ordered the doctor.

Vivien's skin was turning gray. I had seen this when my stepmother died of cancer. Hours before she died her body already looked like a corpse. You could tell her spirit was gone. She was no longer human.

More medical staff came and went. Originally I'd told myself that if we could just make it to the hospital, everything would be okay. Now I felt my life ending. My daughter was about to die, and I knew my marriage would be over if that happened. My mother's first son died at the age of five, and she died with him that day. She gave up wanting to live. The shadow of my dead brother always loomed large, and I'd had to live with that my entire youth, my entire life. I knew the same would happen to Nicole if she lost our daughter. There would be no reason for me to live either.

The machines beeped and whirred, keeping track of Vivien's vital signs. Her heartbeat grew fainter. Her breathing slowed . . . and then stopped. The sound in the room was the same as in the movies. A flatline. Cardiac arrest.

After a million years, a nurse brought in a plastic box and the doctor took out the paddles. The defibrillator buzzed. He waited for it to charge.

One one thousand, two one thousand, three one thousand, four one thousand, five one thousand, six one thousand, seven one thousand ...

I shut my eyes. My tears fell onto her bed. I bit down on my tongue. *If there's a God, He'd goddamn well better help me.*

The doctor moved the paddles into position again, ready to administer a second charge.

"Look!" Nicole exclaimed.

Vivien's left arm twitched. She gasped for air. The doctor looked surprised.

Then my baby opened her eyes. She pushed away her oxygen mask fussily, the way she did whenever Nicole tried to brush her hair. "All done now, Mommy?"

Chapter Two
OUR
LOVE STORY

I was born in the unwed mothers' ward at White Memorial Hospital in East Los Angeles. My biological mother, a twenty-one-year-old from Boston, kept me for three days and then gave me up for adoption to Pat and Marybeth Knox. I went home to a large house in Pasadena, California. I attended kindergarten at Hamilton Elementary School, but my mother was afraid of the busing system and sent me to a Catholic school for the next eight years.

Mine was a good childhood. I played with other children on the block for long hours. We rode bikes, dug holes in the ground, and made forts. Later, I attended San Marino High School. I had a hard time adjusting to being a teenager. My grades were bad. I was thrown off the golf team for fighting. High school. My parents never spoke of my adoption. It was taboo. My father and I were both tall and slim, with brown hair and blue eyes. After her fifth Scotch and soda, my mother liked to joke that I looked exactly like my dad.

Lucky for me I was adopted into privilege and wealth— private schools, summer homes, yacht clubs, tennis clubs, beach clubs, dinner clubs, polo clubs, and country clubs. We had housekeepers; my friends had servants and body-guards. I drifted through high school with the ennui of the entitled, hanging out with skaters and stoners. Most of my friends didn't graduate from high school.

The day after I graduated from high school, my dad walked out on the marriage—he literally went to play golf and never came home.

In a way I couldn't blame him. I was surprised he'd hung on for so long. Maybe he had another woman any-way; he ended up remarrying a year after he left us. The house I grew up in was sold in the divorce, and my sister and I moved in with my mom to a condo in Sierra Madre, a wealthy enclave north of Pasadena. It was a peaceful lit-tle town where the original *Invasion of the Body Snatchers* was filmed in 1956. It was clear that the combination of high school graduation and my parents' divorce had had a similar effect on me. I was depressed and useless. I slept most days, refused to find a job, and barely went to class at Pasadena City College where I was enrolled. For those two years I did one positive thing—I went to a lot of act-ing auditions. Television shows, movies, commercials, I didn't care. My hero was William Holden. I auditioned for a television show with Robert Mitchum, but the role went to actor Nick Stahl. It was after that audition that I told myself I didn't have a passion for acting. When my acting fell by the wayside, there was truly nothing left of me but a depressed lump.

One weekend a friend invited me to go to Santa Barbara, two hours north of Los Angeles. Santa Barbara had the beach and mountains. I loved it. It made me feel human again.

So impulsively, I moved to Isla Vista, an unincorporated community on the beach next to the University of California, Santa Barbara campus. I stayed for five years.

While there, I attended Santa Barbara City College and also took a few classes at UCSB. I supported myself mostly by working at night as a security guard so I could attend classes during the day. One place I worked security was the Paseo Nuevo mall on State Street in downtown Santa Barbara. The city was beautiful, but the population was mostly college kids and retired people. I was twenty-four and felt old. Clearly I needed to move on.

I moved back to Los Angeles to finish college at Cal State University, Northridge. I graduated two years later, with a degree in sociology, supporting myself meanwhile with another security job, at ARCO headquarters in downtown Los Angeles.

It was during this time that I met Nicole—again. The first time was through her cousin when I was sixteen and she was thirteen. She had just broken her hip and was hobbling around on crutches. I didn't pay much attention to her.

The next time I saw her was three years later. She was sixteen, wearing a tight red dress, tall and slender with long brown hair. Her eyes are greenish-brown. She is smart, with a wicked sense of humor; she could and still can really make me laugh. She is Swedish, Irish, and Mexican. Gorgeous. But she had a boyfriend—a scrawny-looking kid who couldn't even drink the beer I offered him. At that age, anyone who didn't drink beer was a loser in my eyes. A year later I found myself with a friend at Nicole's house for a Christmas party. We flirted. She took me outside to the three-story tree house her father had built her years earlier, overlooking a golf course where the benighted football hero O.J. Simpson used to play—after he was tried for the murders of his wife, Nicole Brown Simpson, and a local waiter. The sign on the tree house could be read all the way from the tee box: *Nicole's Tree House*. Nicole's father would sit in the tree house drinking beer. When he'd see O.J., he liked to scream: "I'm at Nicole's house, buddy!" You get a picture of the kind of guy my father-in-law is. Likes to have fun. Likes to do it at the expense of others.

Up in the tree house my own beautiful Nicole, now almost eighteen, and I kissed for the first time.

It was magical. Instantly I was totally in love.

And then, suddenly, her mom was standing there!

What do you two think you're doing?

Busted!

For years it was rumored that her father had chased me down the block with a rifle, but truly, it was her mom you needed to be afraid of.

Nicole's path and mine crossed now and then over the next seven years, but circumstances did not allow us to connect. I say that because I had a lot of growing up to do as I drifted from Santa Barbara to Northridge to Venice

Beach to Pasadena. All the while, I never stopped thinking about Nicole.

The thing was, girls never seemed to like me much. At least that's the experience I'd had so far in my life. I was always the invisible guy. I was the guy to whom the girl— my "friend"— cried to about the boyfriend who'd been cheating on her for the past year. Have you ever been in that position? Confidant to the one you're dying to lean over and kiss?

Then, when I was twenty-seven and I was home for the holidays, I ran into Nicole in the hallway at her aunt's house on Christmas Eve. Normally I would have been too shy to talk to her, but this time I don't know what came over me. I said hello and we started to talk, and before I'd known it, we'd talked all night. In the morning I went home to my family's place for Christmas Day with her phone number in my pocket. It was the first time in my life that I didn't care about the presents under the tree. I called her that day. She was literally the first girl I had *ever* asked out. I'd always known I was going to marry her. Now I was sure.

We dated for several months. Then one day I got up the nerve to tell her that I loved her.

At first, she chose to ignore the three little words that are so hard to say for the first time. I figured maybe she hadn't heard. She was legally deaf, wore hearing aids.

"I love you," I said again.

"I know," she said, slightly irritated. "I heard you. That's nice."

She patted me on the head like a dog.

It wasn't until a month later that she told me she loved me, too. I guess she had to think about it for a while.

Clearly, to the uneducated eye, I had a lot more cons than pros on my list.

But I ended up finding a happiness with Nicole that I never thought I would have. A happiness that this poor, self-hating adopted boy thought he'd never reach.

I proposed to Nicole on her birthday, on top of the tree house where we had kissed for the first time. I gave her a diamond ring passed down from my great-great-grandmother, along with a mosaic I had made that read "MARRY ME." My hope was that we could take the mosaic and cement it in the backyard of our first home.

Thankfully, Nicole said yes. We set out planning the wedding. Nicole was Catholic, and I considered myself a Buddhist. In order to be married in the Catholic Church, I had to convert—or at least promise that I would convert. I figured I could wing it. We had to take classes, and if the priest thought we were doomed from the start, we would be sent to a marriage retreat. We also had to take a test. The test was a hundred multiple-choice questions. I wasn't very good at taking tests.

In the end, the priest gave us his blessing and we were married at Saint Bernadine's Catholic Church in Woodland Hills by Father Robert McNamara, originally from Ireland. The ceremony was an hour-and-a-half long, much longer than any church service I had ever attended.

Afterward, we took a limo to Woodland Hills Country Club for the reception. It was raining. I thought it was a bad omen, but Nicole assured me it was good luck. We were greeted by a mariachi band that arrived bloody and bruised after surviving a car accident. It was Nicole's mother who'd insisted on the mariachi band. To this day I don't know why.

We were seated at a tiny table for two. Father Mac, who performed the ceremony, sat with us. I thought it was a nice touch. Spanish dancers entertained us, as did a Tom Jones impersonator. The DJ filled the room with music, and the guests danced and drank until it was time to go home. It was a wonderful experience. The kind you'd want to watch on video every couple of years.

The next day we arrived at Los Angeles Airport three hours before our flight to our dream honeymoon on Maui. I was looking forward to getting drunk and reading the *Los Angeles Times*. On that very day, the newly organized TSA had taken over the responsibility for airport security. Apparently, someone had walked through the metal detectors with a toy gun and TSA had shut down the entire terminal.

We waited in line for three hours only to be told that we would miss our flight because we were too late to board.

After much red tape and more waiting in line, we were escorted down a long hallway and boarded onto a plane headed to Kauai. It wasn't where I wanted to go, but it was at least in the right direction.

Five hours later we landed in Kauai. We took a taxi to the Sheraton Hotel and checked into our room. For some reason housekeeping had failed to clean up from the last guests. There was beer on the floor, wet towels, and used condoms, a whole yucky scene. We went back down to the front desk.

Finally, we got our room and unpacked. I opened the minibar, got a beer and a bag of sour cream and onion potato chips, and laid down on the bed to watch TV. Nicole came out of the bathroom holding her hair dryer. Then, she looked at me in horror.

"What happened to your eye?"

"What do you mean?"

"It's lopsided."

I looked in the bathroom mirror. My right eye was swollen several times its normal size. A piece of onion powder from the chip got in my eye and caused an allergic reaction.

Nicole called the front desk and they sent a doctor to the room.

I had to wear a patch over my right eye for the entire next week.

Chapter Three
IT'S A GIRL

Nicole's water broke while she was having lunch with my mother. I was at work in South Central Los Angeles—to be precise, I was listening to a recovering heroin addict speak to a room full of parolees about living homeless in some bushes in a park, a fairly regular activity in my day as a parole agent.

I parked my car at Henry Mayo Hospital. The room was nice. It was larger than I expected, and Nicole had it to herself; the $600 a month I was paying for health insurance seemed worth every penny. Nicole was calm, lying on the hospital bed. That morning, she'd told me she felt fourteen months pregnant. She'd asked for the umpteenth time if her nose looked big. I said it looked fine, but honestly, for some reason the women in her family exhibit signs of exponential nose growth during their pregnancies. She'd joked that our baby must be trying to climb out the wrong way, through her sinuses.

A nurse came into the room and checked on Nicole. She was only three centimeters dilated, which meant we had plenty of time for me to run home and get the video camera, some magazines, a cell phone charger, and Nicole's suitcase.

As I drove back to the hospital, I thought of nothing but our baby. I had already seen her; we'd paid out of our own pockets for a fancy color ultrasound from a private facility. With the usual kind of ultrasound insurance paid for, the image was black and white, and the baby could be seen only from the side. With the fancy variety, at a cost of $120, we were able to see our baby from every angle—top, bottom, and sides. The funny thing was, we'd had to return to the place four different times to get our pictures. For some reason, our baby always had her feet pulled up, hiding her face. Maybe she was shy? Mostly she just looked like a golden blob of goo, but I was blown away to learn that she was a *she*. *Oh my God*. We are having a baby girl!

Family and friends came and went. My mother and sister-in-law stayed in the room. Everyone else waited in the hallway.

Despite all those coaching/partnership birthing classes, no one tells you that the father's role in this whole process is virtually non-existent. In the end, there I was, standing like a jackass, holding a video camera to shoot an event I had no intention of ever watching again. The only word I was allowed to utter was "breathe"—like who *wouldn't* be breathing deeply at a moment like this? I could have said "breathe" over the phone. It finally made sense to me why my father was off playing golf when I was born in 1972; he knew he wasn't needed.

It got dark. Nurses came in the room and checked Nicole's vital signs. They changed her IV, listened with a stethoscope, and then the doctor gave her an epidural. Nicole had gone back and forth on the issue of natural childbirth. She didn't want to take any drugs, but I insisted it was a good idea. I wanted her to take all the drugs she could get her hands on to make the birth as brief and painless as possible. I loved her. I didn't want to see her in any pain. There was no need for heroics, I argued, and in the end she agreed. We'd have plenty of time for heroic parenting over the next eighteen years.

The contractions came more frequently and grew more intense. I was exhausted just watching her. I wanted to lie down next to her and hold her. I felt powerless. I stood by the bed holding her hand, trying not to get in the way of the two nurses. Nicole wanted water; I fed her ice chips. My best friend was in pain (and I'd helped to cause that), and all I had to help was ice chips.

"You can do it," I whispered.

It sounded stupid. Of course she could do it. She didn't have a choice. There was no turning back now. The baby was coming. The contractions got stronger, and Nicole's face was red with exertion. I tried to distract myself, but I confess: at one point I thought I was going to faint, though I may have just been foggy from the cough medicine I'd taken when I was home; I'd been suffering a mild flu for the past few days. Clearly, Nicole was much stronger than

I was, and I loved her for it. I was the one who couldn't handle it.

The machines beeped more rapidly. Alarms sounded on the heart monitor. I began to panic. We'd been there for hours, and the doctor hadn't even shown up yet. I couldn't imagine what he was doing.

At last the doctor strolled in looking fresh and rested. He sat on a stool between Nicole's legs and went to work. I pretended to film the birth, but honestly, I wasn't feeling so well. I kept the lens pointed at the wall. Later, I'd tell Nicole that the camera broke. Did we really need film?

At last, it happened. The baby was delivered and swaddled in a blanket. We'd already decided on a name: Vivien Leigh, from *Gone with the Wind,* Nicole's favorite movie. Now she looked into the eyes of the child she'd carried to term. "I love you so much, Vivien."

The day before, Nicole and I had been a couple. Now, all of a sudden we were a *family.*

And it felt as if we'd gone to heaven.

Chapter Four

MOOFISH

Minutes after Vivien was born she was given a battery of tests. Nicole has been hard of hearing since age three because of a series of ear infections that damaged her eardrums. She wore hearing aids. All through the pregnancy, Nicole prayed that Vivien would not be similarly challenged. Right after her birth, we waited nervously for results of a hearing test. When the results came back, we were overjoyed. Our baby had perfect hearing.

At the hospital, Nicole was moved into another room; a nurse showed her how to breast-feed and how to swaddle the baby. Tiny mittens were put on Vivien's hands so she wouldn't scratch her face, and a little beanie was placed on her banana-shaped head. I bought the nurses doughnuts and handed out Starbucks gift cards. We felt well taken care of at Henry Mayo Hospital.

That night as Nicole breast-fed, she observed that Vivien's skin looked dark.

"She looks fine to me," I said. "She just looks tan."

"She shouldn't be tan. Something's wrong."

"She's a quarter-Mexican. Your side of the family, right? I'm sure it's perfectly normal."

I was wrong. I was always wrong every time I was hopeful. Tests revealed Vivien had jaundice; her liver wasn't functioning properly. The hospital didn't consider jaundice life-threatening. They said we could treat Vivien at home with something called a Billi Bed, a three-foot-long lamp that laid across the crib, kind of a *de-tanning* bed for babies. Instead of a cute mobile with animals hanging over her crib, Vivien would have something different to start her life in our happy home. Whatever. At least we were home.

The next day, the nurse pushed Nicole and Vivien in a wheelchair to the front exit while I got the car. I parked in front and stumbled out of the car. Wow, this was really happening.

"Don't we get like a pamphlet or something?" I asked.

The nurse looked back at me. "What for?"

"It's just, well, I have no idea what I'm doing. There should be an instruction manual, don't you think? "

"I think you'll do just fine. Most people forget the car seat."

Childbirth is a strange event. You show up to the hospital with two people, and leave with three. (Sometimes you might leave with eight children, and get a reality show out of it.) You catch yourself every couple of minutes wondering where the heck that baby came from. Just two weeks before Vivien was born I was drinking beer and watching *The Sopranos* with this cool dude Chester Bennington from the band Linkin Park at his condo in Pacific Palisades. Now I was a father slinging diapers and rubber nipples. *Yikes.*

Nicole was on maternity leave for seven months from her marketing job with a cruise line. She liked her job because it was close to home, and because they gave her discounts on cruises—that somehow we never took.

As for me, I was on leave, too. I had plenty of time off from my job in South Central Los Angeles as a parole agent. When Nicole and I decided to have a child, her one request was that I quit my job as a prison guard, a job I'd held for five years. The prison demanded odd hours; I always missed holidays and birthdays because I was low in seniority. As a parole agent I held regular hours and wouldn't be away from my family. But it's funny. I've always been a screwup … unless I put my mind to something. I sometimes end up surprising myself. It's like, wow, man I really got this done.

The first few days of Vivien's life were focused on remedying the situation of her mustard-colored skin. We even placed her next to the window hoping she would retain some vitamin D from the sunshine. The Billi Bed arrived hours after we got home, and came with no instructions. We found ourselves scouring the Internet for information so that we wouldn't inadvertently turn our baby into a Frito.

We also had to take her to get her blood tested daily for the first two weeks. It was hard watching strangers draw blood from my child as she screamed in pain. But days later Vivien was back to normal, and we hunkered down in our bedroom with her, deep into our new life.

Nicole barked orders at me from our queen-size bed. Her emotions swung from serenity and bliss to doom and gloom. I think Tom Cruise needs to send more flowers to Brooke Shields for telling her that postpartum depression isn't real. It is. I know, because we have been there.

As a husband, I quickly got my promised rude awakening. Beyond my ability to serve the nuclear unit, I was insignificant. I was the guy who fetched the remote control. My king-of-the-castle fantasies went right into the diaper hamper, but I didn't mind. Everything for me was about the baby, too. She was our sole focus. Friends and family came and went. They dropped off gifts, as did the UPS man. The living room was filled with gift boxes, the kitchen and the fridge filled with food from thoughtful friends who'd been in our place before. They knew we were strung out like drug addicts from lack of sleep, and were just too beat to cook meals or leave the house. Meanwhile, we avoided the outside world and transitioned into Baby Mode.

Vivien slept in a white bassinet next to our bed. When she slept, I checked on her every ten minutes to see whether she was still breathing. I didn't believe she could do anything on her own. How could she live without the umbilical cord? I feared everything could go wrong at any second.

Nicole breast-fed every hour and a half. She groaned at having to get up while I slept. But I didn't have what Vivien wanted.

Going through life, meeting people with nicknames (many in the context of law enforcement and incarceration), I used to always wonder about the etymology of the different ones I've heard. How is it that someone's parents or siblings start calling a kid they named Adrien or John by a different name? And not just any nickname. A nickname like Stench? Or Scooter? Or what have you. Where does that come from?

Well now I no longer wonder. God help me: in the early days of Vivien's life, Nicole and I gave her a nickname, too.

Somehow our beautiful new baby spontaneously became known to us as Moofish.

It was silly, but heartfelt. And perfectly fitting for those early days of our daughter's life, when everyone in the household was focused most extensively on two things: Nicole's breast milk and Vivien's mouth—which reminded us somehow of a fish in an aquarium, puckering and latched.

Moofish.

One afternoon, half out of our minds from lack of sleep, my darling wife and I had a long conversation that ended in our resolution to change the nickname to Little Moo, lest she discover at a later age the derivation of her moniker.

Early on, fatherhood felt to me at times like living in a haunted house. Vivien could scream and shriek for hours on end. I would hide in various parts of the house, hoping Nicole could soothe her. For the record, most of the time I was always willing but not really wanted. But even Nicole had a limit. That's when I'd call in my training as a prison guard. I could stand anything.

When the crying got to be too much for my wife, I'd take our Little Moo into the bathroom and turn on the ceiling fan. At first I'd hoped the fan would drown out the crying, just to give Nicole a little respite. But I soon realized that the loud whooshing/whirring sound actually soothed Vivien. Someone had given us a baby basket with a thick layer of lamb's wool inside. It fit perfectly between the toilet and the tub.

When Vivien wailed for long periods of time, I would whisper sweet things in her ear, I would talk to her, I would ask, "Why do you cry so much?" That's the really tough thing about babies you don't realize before they're here. They have no display panel. No troubleshooting mechanism. No way to tell you what is ailing them. I've never felt so powerless. In the face of her unhappiness, I was also like a baby, helpless to do anything.

I made up words like "chicka-boka-boo," and sang songs. She didn't understand me, but I videotaped several question-and-answer sessions so that one day we could look back and laugh. Sometimes Vivien would scream herself back to sleep, and I would read for a while until it was time to feed her again.

Sometimes, sitting on the floor, I would think about fatherhood. I'd have these times of reflection, these *How the heck did I get here?* moments. It's funny. I always wanted children. I'm not sure why.

At the same time I kind of never liked kids, even as I was kind of drawn to them—and oddly, I've always been the guy who babies loved.

I guess this has something to do with the fact that when I was twelve years old I actually *dropped a* baby.

Well, not dropped it, exactly.

See, it was summer and I was on a swing in my best friend's backyard. We had been swimming in his pool all day. I don't remember how this happened but suddenly someone put somebody's six-month-old sister in my lap, and I was taken by surprise... and fell backward, the baby with me.

Now, I swear, nobody was hurt. My body acted as a cushion, the baby landed on my stomach and chest. Neither of which were exactly rock hard at that age. And I don't really remember any trauma coming of the whole incident—maybe the mom was mad at me but everybody knew it wasn't my fault.

But since I'd become a dad, well, it was like I had post-traumatic stress. At all costs I had to protect my baby lest history repeat itself.

And Shelby, wherever you are, I am sorry I dropped you.

Chapter Five

PINK BUNNY

Of course every new father knows about all the stuff you have to buy . . . I got a crash course in Baby Bling 101 weeks before the birth. I never questioned where Nicole came up with her facts. Like a Bible, she took to carrying around the well-known book, *What to Expect When You're Expecting*. To Nicole it was the Bible of Breeding. Like all new dads, I vowed to read it, but never quite got around to doing so. Whatever Nicole said, I just took her word for it.

One of the first boondoggles was the baby proofing. We went to a popular chain store. Good Lord. Aisles and aisles full of highly necessary stuff, all of it a fortune.

"What do we need a baby camera for?" I asked.

"So we can see the baby?"

"But she'll be in the next room. Where's she's going to go? Out clubbing?"

Nicole gave me the "you're a such moron" look and we continued down the aisle. She placed a breast pump in the basket. I checked the price.

"Three hundred dollars?! Can't we get a used one on eBay?"

"I'm not sticking my boobs in some used machine."

"We'll sterilize it."

She ignored me. I kept quiet. I never won any protest when it came to the baby products. We needed them and that was that.

Thanks to the generosity of friends and family, we already had enough stuff to start a store of our own. We had stuffed animals, pajamas, blankets, towels, shoes, towels with hoods, hats, shirts, pants, jewelry, cups and saucers, whistles, bells, bowls, clothing, gates, fences, toilet seat alarms, baskets, and diapers.

In the baby-products race, two items came out ahead of the pack. The first was the baby swing. No one ever told me about the baby swing. If I ever get a chance I would like to shake the hand of the person who invented the baby swing. I envision a man like me. Simple and desperate.

The baby swing was magical. I've told you about all the crying. Well, the moment I put Vivien in the swing she passed out cold. It was faster than general anesthesia. Thus the swing became my golden ticket to parenthood. Or maybe it was the tool I needed. A man needs to control things. To do so, he usually needs a tool. As a charter male, I had a garage full of them. But none could stop my baby crying … until the magic baby swing.

More important to my daughter was a small pink Carter's plush bunny that rattled when you shook its head. The top half was a bunny face, the bottom half was a small blanket.

The "blanky" or "manky" or "me-me" is a staple of any childhood. I still have mine, a red blanket with a toy soldier on it. My blanky protected me from the monsters in the closet. It came in handy when my father took me to see *Jaws* at the age of three.

I also had a bunny that sang me lullabies at bedtime. It had a key in the back that wound up a music box inside. Vivien loved her Bunny, but she wasn't very good to Bunny. Sometimes she would drop Bunny while she was in her stroller, or toss him behind the TV, where he'd get covered with dust. At bedtime we would always be searching frantically for Bunny. Vivien would not sleep until Bunny was found.

On Easter Sunday, when Vivien was a year old, we went to the park near our home so Vivien could watch the other children hunt for eggs and I could get out of the house.

After we left the park, we were getting organized by our car. As I put the stroller in the trunk I suddenly noticed— Bunny was gone! I didn't want to say the word "Bunny" in front of the baby. Vivien couldn't read or write, but she knew damn well what "Bunny" meant.

"I've got to go back to the park," I told Nicole.

"What for?" asked Nicole.

"We've got a problem. Someone is not here."

"What are you talking about?" Nicole asked.

I mouthed the words. Nicole could read lips, because of her near-deafness. It came in handy all the time. Her eyes widened and her mouth dropped.

"Hurry!" she admonished

I was frantic. Pure adrenaline.

When I was seven, I lost a toy truck at Burton Chase Park in Marina del Rey. All these years later the memories came pouring back. I'd been devastated—for years I'd gone back to the same sandbox searching for my toy truck, an eighteen-wheeler with the Jolly Green Giant on the side. It was funny how much I loved that truck, which came free when you bought twenty cans of peas and mailed in the labels, something they used to do a lot back in the day. You could actually use the truck as a serving dish; it came with a little brochure picturing the truck filled with peas. Looking back I don't know why anyone would take pleasure in filling up a truck with peas but I ate a lot of peas that year and I loved that truck, even though my father thought it was a "cheap gimmick from the company to make you eat more peas."

I thought about my truck as I ran around the park frantically searching for Bunny. I retraced our steps. I checked under the tree where we'd been sitting. At the concession stand, under the baseball bleachers, the picnic tables.

Asking everyone I saw, "Have you seen a small pink bunny?"

People looked at me like I was a nut case. In my panic I even called out: "Bunny!"

It was like she was part of the family.

A damn important part, as every parent learns.

I walked across the grass toward the restrooms, scanning the ground as I went, remembering how they'd taught me some of the techniques of searching at the academy. I had hunted down hundreds of wanted felons but now I needed to find a pink bunny and it was eluding me. I felt like I was at a low point of my life. I'd let my family down. Both of my girls would hate me forever if I couldn't find Bunny.

I turned around in a circle, slowly scanning the park.

And then I noticed something.

Near the exit. Sitting on the fence. Something was sitting on top of the left pole. Something pink.

Bunny!

When we got home, I went immediately to my computer and started searching eBay. Miraculously, there were two other Carter's pink plush bunnies listed. Clearly, the item was nearly extinct. It hadn't been manufactured in years. There seemed to be few if any left. A bidding war ensued. My adversaries were Irma1957 from Minnesota and Carl-Bigalow46 from Maine. They had no idea who they were dealing with.

I printed the bunny page and taped it to the wall. All my determination and power was focused on obtaining those two remaining bunnies. I knew in the end I would be victorious, because a little girl's happiness depended on me.

I started off the bidding at five dollars. Irma1957 quickly countered with five dollars and twenty-six cents.

Odd, right? How had she arrived at that? Clearly I was dealing with a madwoman.

Then CarlBigalow46 raised the stakes with a maverick bid of fifteen dollars and seventy-five cents.

Nicole thought I was being silly and spending too much. To me, this was an investment in our future sanity. Never again would we have to worry about losing Bunny.

I told Nicole I'd take a second job if I had to, just to win the eBay bid. And then I bided my time, ready to make my play.

The bidding was slated to end at three in the afternoon on a particular day. I took the day off work. I counted down the hours and then the minutes, clicking the mouse and refreshing the computer screen. The bid amount never changed.

With one minute left, I punched in a bid for twenty-five dollars on both sites.

And as time ran out, I became the proud owner of two pink Carter's plush bunnies.

Because you could never be too prepared when it came to Bunny.

Nicole ran into the room and kissed me as if I'd just brought home a check from the lottery. We danced in celebration.

Parenting: you have to take the joy where you can get it.

Chapter Six

A SECOND CHANCE

After her first seizure, Vivien was alive, but her condition was critical.

The doctor thought she might have a brain hemorrhage that could still be bleeding. Nicole had picked her up from her crib at seven a.m.; for all we knew, her seizure could have been going on for hours. I couldn't imagine what my poor baby was going through. According to the doctor, at this point, all of her senses had been stripped away. She had her hearing and her sight, but she didn't have the ability to process what her senses perceived. She was weak and wobbly and unable to sit up on her own.

"She could have irreversible brain damage from the lack of oxygen," the doctor said. He suggested a spinal tap, collecting the cerebrospinal fluid.

The hardest part for me was the fact of Vivien's tender age. Not yet two years old, she wasn't much able to communicate with us in any meaningful way. *"All done now, Mommy?"* Oddly, it had been one of her most complete sentences to date. As she'd developed, Nicole had been concerned as it was that her speech was delayed; we'd even taken her to several speech therapists and we were monitoring her progress.

Now, of course, a little speech delay seemed inconsequential . . . or maybe it was critical? Had we been missing something? At this point everything was up in the air, and Vivien's ocean-blue eyes were distant and hollow. The right side of her body was paralyzed, her face sagged. Normally her lips were full, like a baby Angelina Jolie. Now they were thin and pale. Her chestnut-brown hair was matted down. Her head was pulled to the side like she was caught in a G-force.

They needed to run more tests. They wanted to give her an angiogram to outline the blood vessels in her brain. They drew blood, took X-rays, and ordered a CT scan. Nicole stood inside the imaging room while I stood beside Vivien. My daughter cried, screamed, and thrashed. I held her down as I was asked. I knew she was screaming for me to save her. I couldn't bear her screams, but I couldn't blame her either. Here I was, helping to shove her inside a giant scary CT tube. Some dad.

The doctor came in and put his arm around me. His body language communicated the seriousness of the situation. He led me over to a computer in the hallway. I didn't know it at the time, but he was trying to prepare me for the worst.

"There's a tumor on the left side. I'm not sure what it is."

He pointed at the computer monitor, to a white dot the size of a pea on the CT scan image of Vivien's brain. I had prayed for her to live but forgotten to pray for her health.

The tumor was on the left side of her brain. That's all he knew. Also, one side of her brain appeared to be half the size of the other. It reminded me of a butterfly with one wing. I wondered: *How do you make a brain grow? Is there a vitamin for that?* I wondered: *Would she ever be a normal girl? Would she ever be able to speak again? Would she even be able to recognize her mother or father? Would she have anything even remotely near a normal life?*

Henry Mayo Hospital didn't have a child neurology unit, so Vivien was transferred to Children's Hospital in Los Angeles, on Sunset Boulevard. She was placed in a car seat and strapped onto a gurney. The gurney was locked in place for the thirty-minute ambulance ride. The paramedics were great. They were kind and gentle with Vivien, and put Nicole and me at ease.

Nicole went in the ambulance and I followed behind with my father in law. He was the last person I wanted to be with, but I was happy to be with anyone. I felt so alone.

"It's going to be all right," he said.

I needed to hear that, even if it wasn't true. Even if I didn't believe it, it was comforting.

At Children's Hospital I argued with the intake coordinator.

"I can't admit anyone without authorization," she said.

I restrained myself from bashing her over the head with my chair.

"I have my two-year-old strapped to a gurney being pushed by two paramedics. What more do you need?"

"I need the proper hospital paperwork. You're missing the admittance form. We have a system here."

My faith in the medical system began to die that day, an agonizing process at once swift and drawn-out. I had been hospitalized only once, for an appendectomy, when I was a teenager. I had my eighteenth birthday at Huntington Hospital in Pasadena. It had seemed so easy back then. My dad had taken me, and they admitted me right away. I shared a room with an old man who had testicular cancer. We watched *Knight Rider* together, cheering David Hasselhoff. The old man told me he'd had his appendix taken out when he was eighteen—on *his* birthday. Another patient limped in and gave me a button that said "Happy Birthday." He died the next day of a brain tumor.

"So, there's nothing you can do to help my two-year-old daughter?" I asked.

"Not without the proper paperwork."

There was one thing I knew about red tape: there is always a way to cut through it. I called a family friend, an ear, nose, and throat doctor at University of Southern California Hospital. Dennis was good friends with Nicole's parents and he was always there to lend us medical advice.

My mother-in-law had already notified him about Vivien's seizure, and he got back to me in two minutes.

"Go straight up to intensive care," Dennis said.

The inside of the building was dirty and old. The hallways were jammed with sick children waiting to be admitted. I had heard such glowing advertising about Children's

Hospital of Los Angeles, and I was kind of shocked. We were met in the hallway by a cocky young doctor; he wore a diamond stud in one ear. We were placed in a room. Vivien lay on her mother's chest in a daze. I kissed her and tried to get her to smile, but she was clearly drained. Normally I could have her laughing in no time.

Family members arrived. My mother brought us each a change of clothes. Up until then we had basically been wearing the clothes we'd slept in—Nicole's T-shirt said, "I love hot moms." I'd given it to her as a joke for her birthday. My shirt said, "I got a black belt in crazy." Later we would throw away the clothes from that day. They felt unlucky, a reminder of a bad time when we entered through a gateway and onto the difficult path with epilepsy that we are still traveling.

The cocky young doctor came back into the room. "There's really nothing to worry about," he assured us. "It was just a fever seizure. Very common in children her age."

I wanted to believe him. He was the one with the medical degree. But I had seen the pictures of Vivien's brain. You didn't have to be a medical genius to know that something was wrong.

"But fever seizures only last one to two minutes. This seizure was much longer. It could have been hours," said Nicole quoting from information Googled on her iPhone.

"We were told she has a tumor," I added.

The doctor rolled his eyes. "It was a fever seizure, believe me. I know what I'm talking about. I'm discharging her."

I called my friend Dennis again. He got us admitted overnight.

When the young doctor returned to our room, clearly

he was furious.

"I don't know what you think you're doing," he said, "but *I* know that there's nothing wrong with your daughter."

I was in no mood for a pissing match. Nicole, who is half-Mexican, was giving me her Aztec death look. I was ready to mop the floor with this little twerp, but I knew Vivien needed help; I would be little help from a jail cell. "Imagine if she were your daughter," I implored. "Could you just observe her for a little longer? Something's really wrong here and we need to get it figured out."

Something in my plea seemed to reach him. His face relaxed into a look of acceptance. He turned and left the room.

An hour later we were taken upstairs to the pediatrics neurology wing. It was dark and cold—the air-conditioning was powerful to keep bacteria from proliferating. There were babies not much older than six months lying in wooden cribs that looked like cages, completely enclosed. The doors to the rooms were closed, but the babies could be seen through windows. It was early evening. There were no other parents around. Most of the children seemed alone. The whole scene jerked at my heart.

A team of medical people came in and out of our room asking a wide range of questions.

"Did the baby drink any household chemicals or poisons?"

"Is there a history of seizures in the family?"

"Did she fall down or injure her head?"

We repeated the same story to each new doctor: "We found her in her crib having a seizure."

Finally they left us alone and we all got some

sleep—Nicole on the bed with Vivien on her chest, me on a chair beside the bed. It was uncomfortable, but we were in the hospital, we felt safe. The worst appeared to be over.

The next day was Vivien's second birthday. While Vivien and Nicole slept, I went downstairs to the gift shop and bought birthday presents. She was supposed to be having a party today, but obviously we'd had to cancel it. I got her a Polly Pocket, a little doll that comes with an extra set of clothes and accessories. I also bought a princess coloring book, a stuffed bear, and a purse shaped like a dog. For Vivien's ten-year-old roommate, Eddie, I purchased a set of Batman action figures. Eddie had epilepsy and his parents apparently were not so good at keeping up with his medication.

When I got back, Vivien was sitting up and playing with Nicole. Squealing with delight, the birthday girl ripped open her Polly Pocket. We could see she was slow using her right arm but we were glad she was alive, moving around and laughing.

Pretty soon we ran into our next round of red tape. Since Vivien was conscious, her care was being bumped down to outpatient status. She would be released and referred to our pediatrician to get a referral for an MRI and an EEG. Since we had our health insurance with an HMO, every referral had to be cleared through our pediatrics doctor, even though she knew nothing about neurology. We were discharged.

Driving home, we were just past Mulholland Drive on the congested 405 Freeway when Vivien vomited in the car. The motion was making her sick, we figured. Nicole sat in the back holding a plastic bag in front of our Little Moo.

The vomiting continued after we got home. Each time Vivien drank or tried to eat, she immediately threw up. She threw up so much that we ran out of towels, sheets, and blankets. Because our pediatrician was on vacation—another stroke of bad luck—we had to speak to the on-call doctor, who seemed to think the vomiting was normal. Vivien didn't look normal.

"She should be fine," the doctor said, but when she still wasn't better by the evening, we drove back to Henry Mayo Hospital. This time I parked at the emergency exit and waited until the emergency doors opened. We weren't going to wait in line. We had already been there the day before. I felt like they owed us.

The door opened and a policeman walked out, pulling a scruffy man in handcuffs. Nicole made a dash for the door, holding Vivien, and approached a woman sitting at a computer. I felt relieved to be back at the hospital. I parked the car and came back through the front door. I was stopped by security and had to get a pass. I ran down the hall and found Nicole lying on a hospital bed holding Vivien.

Some of the medical staff remembered us. The doctors were all different. A young and handsome one introduced himself. He seemed very confident. "I'm going to give her Zofran. That will stop her vomiting."

"But how's it going to work if she keeps throwing up?" Nicole said.

"Trust me. They give it to cancer patients. She's going to be fine."

It was hard to believe a tiny white pill could stop such

carnage. The drug worked, and Vivien was able to drink and eat two hours later. We went home again.

The next day Vivien woke up and she was better. The color had returned to her face and her jaw was no longer sunken in.

Two days later she was running around the house like nothing had happened. Nicole and I were astonished. She was a happy little girl.

The good part, we told ourselves, was that she was too young to remember any of what had happened.

Chapter Seven

INSURANCE SUCKS

I had the same doctor until I was nineteen, a chain-smoking college football player who decided to become a doctor after being injured his senior year at the University of Southern California. He genuinely cared about the families he treated. He also liked to make fun of my father for having gone to UCLA. His office was in an old historic building in Pasadena. Parking was easy, and I never had to wait. I never had to present an insurance card labeled PPO or HMO. No co-payment, either. I just went to the doctor and my family paid my bill.

Then something changed. I walked in one day and the receptionist acted like I was a leper. She couldn't look me in the eye.

"We no longer take your insurance," she mumbled.

"But he's been my doctor my entire life."

"That's our policy."

I left, and for the next few years I didn't have insurance. I didn't think I needed it. I was young and single, and believed I was immortal. I didn't get insurance again until I was twenty-seven, when I became a prison guard.

No one truly understands the medical system until they have to actually use their insurance. As it turns out, my policy was a PPO (Preferred Provider Organization). I took it for granted at the time, but under this plan, we could choose to go to any doctor we wished, as long as they were in the plan. As Vivien grew, we learned more and more, but always in small doses. There were the usual doctor visits, the colds, and flu. When she was nine months old, she cut her finger on a piece of broken glass. But none of it compared to the situation we found ourselves in now.

Once out of the hospital, we were experiencing the medical system on an outpatient basis. When you think about it, medical care has set hours. Mostly we get sick or need medical care when the doctor's office is closed. We are forced to wait in line at the emergency room. Even urgent care closes at nine p.m. The doctor never calls you at home to see how you are doing. You're the one calling the doctor for the test results, until a nurse who you've never met calls to give you the news. If you have any questions, you have to wait for the doctor to call you back. It takes forever.

After waiting an interminable two weeks, we were finally referred to Pediatric Neurology at Children's Hospital in Los Angeles, where we had spent the night after the first seizure. We didn't want to go back there, but there weren't too many choices in children's neurology in Los Angeles. I could change my insurance plan only once a year, in October. The same went for Nicole's insurance through her work. So for now we were stuck with Children's.

Our next major roadblock came from the insurance company. We needed a referral to get an EEG and an MRI. It sounded simple enough, but we hadn't realized how much red tape was involved, even after the doctor requested the tests.

A few more weeks of phone calls and pleading followed—I even sent flowers and a card to suck up to the insurance adjuster who was processing my case.

Finally they granted our doctor's wishes and arranged for Vivien's EEG and MRI to be given . . . at two separate places, 200 miles apart, on the same day.

After more wrangling, we finally got both scheduled at UCLA Hospital in Westwood, an hour from our home.

Once again we were very concerned because Vivien would have to be put under anesthesia for both the EEG and the MRI. She would be subjected to needles and having strange objects placed on her head. Only one parent was allowed to accompany her, so Nicole went in. I knew that Vivien would want to be with her mommy more than with me. To be candid, it was less stressful for me to wait in the lobby than watch my child suffer.

Nicole and I were pleased that the medical staff at UCLA were kind and eager to help. The EEG and MRI went smoothly. We felt like we were finally making progress.

An EEG, or electroencephalography, is the recording of electrical activity along the scalp, and measures fluctuations within the neurons of the brain. The recording takes twenty to forty minutes. The most common use of the EEG is diagnosis of epilepsy, because clear abnormalities in the brain can be recorded. It's also used to identify comas and brain death, and it's the first test used to diagnosis tumors, strokes, or brain disorders.

An MRI, or magnetic resonance imaging, is used to *map* every part of the body, including brain and muscle tissues. The MRI is a device in which the patient lies down and a powerful magnet scans an image of the body. The MRI provides a contrast between soft tissues, and unlike X-rays and CT scans, does not use radiation.

A second EEG was ordered. We got up at four a.m. to avoid rush-hour traffic on the way to Children's Hospital. Our appointment wasn't until seven, but we always had to arrive early and wait; otherwise, our appointment would be canceled. I carried a sleepy Vivien to the car, where Nicole spent the next two hours trying to keep her entertained and awake so that she would sleep through the EEG.

We waited in the lobby for an hour, then were taken to a waiting room where a nurse came in with a wooden box with twenty wires sticking out of it. It looked like a fifth-grader's science project. I couldn't believe they didn't have anything more high-tech than a wooden box. The nurse rubbed Vaseline on the pads and attempted to stick them to Vivien's head, but she kicked and screamed.

It took an hour for the nurse to stick the patches to Vivien's head, and she still never fell asleep. The power in the building went out twice. I was afraid this would interrupt the results.

Then another test was conducted, using flashing strobe lights to determine whether Vivien's seizures were triggered by sight. Patterns of bright flashing lights on the retina can cause seizures. You can find on the Internet many accounts of people having seizures while watching movies and cartoons. It's funny how fast you go from invincible twenty-something to dumbstruck dad. The more you know about the world, the less safe you feel. Now I have to protect her from Disney?

After we had our tests, we were ready to go see the specialist.

Only the next available appointment to see a neurologist at Children's Hospital was… in eight months.

My daughter had died, come back to life, and the soonest we could see a specialist was in eight months. I wanted to scream at the receptionist, but I was getting worn down. I politely asked to be put on a waiting list.

One day the hospital called. There'd been a cancellation! Hallelujah!

Nicole and I both called in sick and took Vivien to Children's. We waited an hour in the waiting room, then another hour inside the examining room. The waiting didn't bother us; we were just happy to have gotten an appointment. Most of the other children waiting in the lobby seemed to be afflicted with serious neurological disorders like cerebral palsy, autism, and Tay-Sachs disease.

At last we met the doctor.

She was in her fifties, and had pink hair.

It threw me off, I have to admit.

What she said threw me even farther: "Your daughter is a very lucky little girl. Her brain injury barely missed her cerebral cortex. She could have been paralyzed for the rest of her life."

"So it's a miracle," said Nicole.

"Yes, I would call it that. A 1 percent survival rate. Let's run some tests."

The doctor proceeded to do some hand-eye coordination tests—it was weirdly comical because some of it reminded me of preschool, and some of it reminded me of the tests police give to suspected drunk drivers. Vivien was encouraged to run up and down the hallway, hop on one leg and then the other. She touched her finger to her nose and then tapped her index finger to her thumb.

Presented with the tests and the exam, the doctor was... stumped.

"We'll just have to wait and see," she said.

Nicole and I just stared at her. Her hair was incredibly pink.

"So that's it?" I said at last.

"What else would you like?"

"I don't know. Some advice, I guess."

"Look, billions of bacteria that we can't see or explain invade the body daily. Too much to wrap our heads around. So when people die, we just call it natural causes. Most people that die are really being attacked by bacteria and their body can no longer fight it. It's a miracle that any of us survive as long as we do. I wouldn't worry about it."

She had a point. I just didn't see it.

"What if she has another seizure? I mean, should we sleep in her room just to make sure?"

"She won't. Only 5 percent of children have another seizure. You can always tie little bells to the corners of her sheets, and if she moves, the bells will go off."

We left with a feeling of utter, abject despair. We wanted to do something, not *nothing*. The doctor was acting as if Vivien had fallen down and scraped her knee. We knew differently. The abject terror of that night of her first seizure will live with me forever.

I was worried about the tumor, which was downplayed to a dried spot of blood. We wanted a second opinion, but the insurance company declined our request.

We decided to pay out of pocket to go see an esteemed doctor at UCLA. Nicole had read about him in the *Los Angeles Times*. He had successfully removed part of the brain of a month-old infant who was having one hundred seizures a day.

We waited for four hours to see the doctor—the standard time, we were learning. I always wonder: Could they not just tell us to come a few hours later? Why do they give appointments? It was a Friday evening, and Vivien was playing outside on the fourth floor of the children's neurology ward. Children's Hospital didn't have an outside playground with slides like UCLA did. It didn't even seem like it was designed for children. UCLA seemed a children's paradise in comparison.

The first thing the doctor did was to walk out onto the playground and watch Vivien play. I liked him immediately. The fact that he would take the time just to observe.

"Have you noticed that she runs with her right arm out to balance herself?"

We hadn't.

"It's very slight, but it's associated with children who have brain injuries. Judging from her scans she has a higher risk of having more seizures. I would recommend putting her on medication."

This new doctor, call him Dr. S, also introduced us to the Charlie Foundation for pediatric epilepsy. It was nice that there was a community of people who understood our struggle and fought against epilepsy. Not only was I excited to hear that there was an alternative, I also knew who the founder, Jim Abrahams, was. He had written and directed my favorite movies, and was a personal hero of mine. My childhood comedy routines were peppered with movie quotes from his movies—*Airplane!*, *The Naked Gun*, *Hot Shots!*, *Top Secret*, and *Kentucky Fried Movie*.

He founded it after his twenty-month-old son Charlie was having multiple seizures a day and still wasn't cured after brain surgery. Jim turned to the Ketogenic Diet, even after it was dismissed by five pediatricians. The Ketogenic Diet, founded in the 1920s, is a high-fat, low-carbohydrate diet with no sugars. Sugar speeds up brain activity. No doctor had ever told us of a diet for children with epilepsy. We had always thought we had to rely on medication alone.

The MRI test results came back, and just as Dr. S had surmised, the most logical explanation was that Vivien had suffered a stroke during her birth. Nicole had done all the right things during her pregnancy. She didn't smoke or drink. She watched what she ate, and took prenatal vitamins. She exercised and got plenty of sleep. But like they say, stuff happens. It has to happen to someone. Unfortunately, it happened to our Vivien. We'd brought her into this world, and we were going to do everything in our power to help her through it.

All the arrows pointed to epilepsy, but he didn't want to say it was a disease until she had more seizures. There was a chance she would never have seizures again and it would just be a condition. Epilepsy is a disease that affects three million people in the United States and fifty million worldwide, according to the Epilepsy Foundation.

"Epilepsy is a brain disorder where a person has repeated seizures," explained Dr. S. "Seizures are events in which brain activity is disrupted, changing behavior and attention."

We were always told to wait, because many doctors were taught that seizures were normal and sometimes healthy for the brain. But we had the Internet and were constantly surfing. New medical studies showed the opposite: that any trauma to the brain was bad.

Looking back, we realized we had seen the seizures mere hours after Vivien was born; we just hadn't known what they were. Once, while I was holding her, and another time, while Nicole was trying to breast-feed her, Vivien moved away and pushed her head back up to the right. Her eyes fluttered and her mouth sort of cringed on the right side. The doctor from Henry Mayo Hospital had insisted that this behavior was normal. He said the baby was just trying to touch the placental sac with her head.

In time it was decided that Nicole had developed a blood clot somewhere in her body during Vivien's delivery, most likely because of the physical strain of childbirth. The blood clot entered Vivien's body, and stopped near her cerebral cortex; just one centimeter further and Vivien would have been permanently paralyzed. The tumor was actually a spot of dried blood that was interfering with her neurons. Now it made sense why hospitals pushed women to get C-sections—so the baby wouldn't suffer brain damage.

We weren't thrilled about putting Vivien on medication, but we wanted to prevent any further seizures. One of the newer drugs we dismissed immediately, because it was linked to tissue damage; we didn't want the medication to impede her development. Vivien's first prescription was for Diastat, a rectal gel used to stop seizures. It worked by calming over-activity in the brain. It came in a pre-filled syringe the size of a turkey baster. The second drug was Clonazepam, used for anxiety disorders associated with depression. It came in a wafer form and dissolved in the mouth. It didn't do much for seizures, but in emergency situations when we didn't have Diastat it was something to give her to slow down the seizure. Nicole could carry them in her purse, and I had them in a tiny capsule attached to my car keys.

The third drug was Keppra, given in liquid form. It was an anticonvulsant that decreased abnormal excitement in the brain. Vivien was given a small dose twice a day. We had to keep a close watch on her height and weight, and adjust the dose each time after she suffered another seizure. The side effects of Keppra were of significant concern. It had been on the market for only a few years, and they didn't know actually why it worked. I soon stopped reading blogs about children experiencing such side effects as depression, hallucinations, seizures, rash, swelling, and weight gain. Each time we gave Vivien a higher dose it took a few weeks for her to adjust; but for the most part she did well with Keppra. She had two side effects. One was weight gain; the other was itching—she would scratch herself all night long while she slept.

One blessing: we liked our new doctor. Dr. S knew how to talk to a couple of very concerned laymen. He was able to put Vivien's illness into perspective. "I take blood pressure medication," he said. "Some people need coffee, others need pills. We all maintain."

Once we got Vivien's medication prescribed it was another battle with the insurance. The insurance company didn't seem to care what the doctor asked for; it was just a recommendation. And the pharmacy didn't want to rock the boat because the insurance company was picking up the tab.

If I had seen little compassion in the medical field, I saw exactly zero at the pharmacy. After several months on Keppra, Vivien started to have seizures again. What we didn't know was that the pharmacy had switched from the Keppra brand medication to a generic. Even when we got a doctor's approval, the insurance company didn't want to cover the name brand. With insurance, the brand name was fifty dollars a bottle, and Vivien needed a bottle every month. I would have paid out of pocket, but the Keppra brand was 600 dollars a bottle.

We'd had two seemingly blissful years with Vivien before her first obvious and serious seizure. I can only imagine how much worrying we would have done if we'd known just after her birth that she was epileptic, or how many constraints we would have placed on her at every stage of her infancy and early childhood.

Now, at last, we had a name for what was going on. Instead of telling family and friends that we didn't know what was wrong with Vivien, we could hang a sign on it: epilepsy.

I had been a sick child, developing asthma at the age of two from being fed rice cereal. My parents were told that I would not live past the age of seven. They took turns holding me next to a hot shower in the bathroom; the steam was supposed to open my lungs. Often I would be awakened by my father, who'd heard me wheezing and gasping for air from down the hall. At times, my mother was too frozen with fear to help me. She couldn't handle the possible loss of another child.

By the age of nine, I was taking nine asthma pills a day and used two different inhalers. By the time I was an adult I no longer needed the pills, but I started and finished one inhaler every other month. My hope was that epilepsy would be just as manageable.

Of course, now that we knew she had epilepsy we had to face the fact that things were *not* going to get better. For now we had to be content with the fact that she wasn't comatose or confined to a wheelchair. It was comforting to know that throughout history people had had meaningful lives with epilepsy: Socrates, Plato, Van Gogh, Julius Caesar, Truman Capote, Napoleon, Peter the Great, Dostoyevsky. We would do our best to carry on for her sake.

That is not to say that, on the day Vivien was diagnosed with epilepsy, our world forever changed.

It's weird to think about it now, but just before Vivien's seizure, life had been looking unusually promising for the first time in my life, to be honest. I had recently had my first art show, an installation of prison weapons, at the Ben Maltz Gallery in Los Angeles. I was attending weekly writers groups and had generated several original TV pilots. I was doing stand-up comedy at the Ice House in Pasadena and The Comedy Store in Hollywood. And I had reached another important juncture in showbiz: I had made it to the "pitch stage" with one of my ideas. Several major television producers wanted meetings.

On the night we found out about Vivien's condition, believe it or not, I had a comedy show to perform. They say good comedy comes from pain. Well I have to tell you: that night, as they say in comedy, I killed.

I rushed home after my set and found Nicole in the bedroom, crying. I grabbed her and held her tight. I vowed right there that my comedy career was over. My place was here, at home. At least for now.

"I'm so sorry this happened to Vivien."

We cried together. We cried a lot. We talked and we held each other and fell asleep hoping the nightmare would go away in the morning.

Of course it did not. In adversity I found strength. I grew more aware of how quickly time passed, and came to cherish every second with my wife and daughter more than ever.

Until that day we got the diagnosis, I'd been coasting through life, always taking the easy route. I'd had some hard times, but I also knew who to fall back on if things got bad. I also had a lot of anger, and was good at blaming others for my problems. Now I realized I couldn't change people; I had to change *myself*. I let go, and for the first time in my life I was at peace. I was no longer obsessed with my problems. I had more important things to worry about. I had Vivien's problems.

That night, I let go. I let go of the things I could not control. I realized that what mattered most to me are my wife and my daughter. I learned for the first time that at any moment we can all have the rug pulled out from under us. Dying is a process of nature, but dying too soon is a tragedy.

I had always thought of myself as a victim. I thought that no one cared about me. I thought that my parents didn't love me enough. To be in control I had to let go of those negative thoughts once and for all. My thinking changed, and my mind became more focused. I was now living in the present. My thoughts were no longer petty. Someday Vivien could at least look back on her life and know that I'd always been next to her; that no matter what, I had done my best not to let her down. I wanted Vivien to know who her father was, just in case she never got the chance. I wanted her to know what mattered to me. What I cared about. What I held dear. I didn't have much to leave in the way of a material legacy, but I wanted to leave *something*. I wanted teachable moments for Vivien when she asked me life questions. Most of all, I wanted her to know that everything would be okay. I had lived a good life and I had found true happiness being her father. I had never done anything profound with my life. Now it was time.

This was a frightening period for Nicole and me. Always in our minds was the fear that Vivien could die at any time.

In a strange way epilepsy brought Nicole and me closer, and showed me what I should value most in life.

I started to write Vivien letters and mail them to her so she would have a record of my thoughts—something to look back on in case I passed away too soon. Nicole opened an email account and we began to send Vivien daily messages, along with pictures, to better capture our feelings. We also did it to remind ourselves of what we struggled through.

In the beginning I looked for support from others, but I never got it. We spent the first few months thinking that she—and we—were facing a death sentence, that she would be brain-damaged and live in a group home. I felt completely and desperately alone with epilepsy.

Then one day after a hospital visit to UCLA I was trying to explain to Vivien why she had to go through all the pain of doctor visits and exams. She was three-and-a-half years old. I wasn't doing a very good job at explaining; I didn't really know what to say. She grabbed my hand as we walked down the hallway, stopped, and looked up at me. "You get what you get, Daddy, so don't throw a fit. The worst you can do is give up." She had so much strength and courage, and she never complained.

I have three suggestions for dealing with any disease. First, try to find the positive side to it. I learned to be grateful that this disease was manageable. It wasn't terminal. I became determined to find out everything about epilepsy.

The Internet was a wonderful source of information, and disinformation. I made as many contacts as I could. I talked to as many doctors, nurses, and medical personnel as I could. Often our greatest help was just bumping into knowledgeable strangers at the park, or walking along the beach.

Second, find support. Any kind of support helps. Someone you can talk to. Don't let the disease run your life; *you* run your life. Learn to manage the disease—don't exhaust yourself, exhaust the disease. Change the way you think. Dr. S said that we couldn't let epilepsy take over our lives, but the truth was that epilepsy had *become* our lives.

And third, get a theme song. Mine was "Eye of the Tiger" by Survivor. If you want, you can borrow it.

Chapter Eight
SERIES OF SEIZURES

The days turned into months, and then a year went by. There were no more seizures; we got on with our lives the best we could. To meet expenses I took a second job, on weekends, working security for a cellular phone company in Santa Monica. It was a thirty-five-mile drive south down the 405 Freeway. It was hard to adjust. I was used to working with the same people and the same routine. Now I felt like I was starting all over, learning a new position and getting to know new people. I felt old. I worked every Sunday, a ten-hour shift. Later, several of Vivien's seizures would occur while I was at my second job. It was a stressful time, but I was doing my best to provide for my family.

We put Vivien in swim and dance classes. She loved to sing and dance, so we made a makeshift stage in our living room and put on shows for anyone who would watch. We played dress up, fashion show, Barbies, and all the other things little girls do.

Vivien seemed to be progressing like any other child. Everyone but us forgot her diagnosis. They couldn't imagine how such a cute little girl could have such an affliction. I basically refused to believe that she wouldn't get better. But no matter what we did, we could not take away the epilepsy or predict when the next seizure would happen. We could take Vivien to all the doctors and specialists in the world, but in the end we were the ones left alone with her. On the outside we were fine, but on the inside we were suffering.

We waited every second of every hour of every day for her next seizure.

We waited in suspended animation for nearly a year after her hospitalization.

Wait for it. Wait for it. Wait for it.

Finally, it happened.

She was three. Sitting on the couch with Nicole one morning. Suddenly she threw up. She lost her ability to communicate. The muscles in her face twitched. Her mouth drooped, and she lost awareness.

Nicole wasn't even sure whether she was having a seizure, because this seizure was different from her first. Nicole moved Vivien to the bedroom and laid her down. She videotaped the seizure, which stopped on its own after a few minutes, without medication.

As we would learn, with each seizure it was as if a sudden squall had developed and rained down on her, leaving her in a helpless, hopeless fog. I started to think of the seizures as Vivien's rain. She was like a little girl alone in a boat in a storm, far out to sea. And there was nothing I could do about it.

At one point, in response to my question, Vivien described her seizures. "It feels like when you drink a cherry Slurpee too fast, Daddy. It's raining in my head."

As if the dam had now broken, the third seizure followed a few weeks later, in February. This time, Vivien had woken up two hours earlier than usual. I put her on the couch in front of the television, turned on cartoons and went into the kitchen to get a cup of coffee. Suddenly, I heard a strange grunting sound, a sound I had never heard. It didn't sound good. I rushed into the living room and found her lying on her back, staring at the wall. My concern this time was that bright or flashing lights from the television had caused the seizure, as they've been known to do. I picked her up. Her pants were wet. I carried her into our bedroom.

"I think she had another seizure," I called.

Once we got to the hospital Vivien began to come around. By the time she was taken for a CT scan she was kicking and screaming. Like last time, I had to hold Vivien down while they shoved her into that big white sarcophagus of a machine.

The day after Christmas, Nicole called me while I was driving a mentally ill parolee to the Social Services office. It was happening again.

The parolee I was with had been in and out of mental institutions her whole life. She was extremely unstable and I didn't know how I was going to tell her that I needed to leave her and drive home. Luckily, I didn't have to say anything; she heard Nicole crying over the phone.

"You can drop me off on the corner, Mr. Knox. I'll walk to the office from there."

I was touched by her compassion. In the past I had had nothing but problems from Lisa, who had a record of smoking crack, prostitution, and robbing liquor stores.

With the onset of the seizure, Nicole had given Vivien Diastat, one of the three drugs we carried with us to stop seizures. Vivien was awake by the time I got to the emergency room. She looked exhausted; as we were beginning to understand, it would take her a few days after each seizure to return to normal. She'd be sluggish for several days, like she was getting over the flu. She'd have no spark. No eye contact. Her emotions would be flat. She'd seem as if she was more observing the world from a distance, not engaging with it.

In time I was given to understand that after each seizure her brain had to adapt in order to recover. In a sense, it was as if she was in another reality—communication at times was difficult. I would ask her a question, but sometimes she wasn't able to understand what I was asking. She'd look at me as if I was speaking a foreign language. It was heartbreaking to watch as she struggled to find the right words and meanings. Her voice was weak, and her words came out in a whisper.

Six months later Vivien awakened at four in the morning and threw up. This had become a warning sign: when she woke up early and vomited, there was a 99 percent chance she would suffer a seizure.

She seemed all right at first, but then she literally walked into a wall. Her balance was off, like she was drunk. Nicole gave her the Diastat, but Vivien's seizure didn't stop. She fell unconscious and we jumped into the car. I dialed 911, hoping to get them to call the hospital and tell them that we had a child en route with a seizure. What I got was a complete surprise.

"Nine-one-one operator, how may I direct your call?"

"My four-year-old daughter is suffering a seizure!"

"Do you need an ambulance?"

"No, I'm driving to the hospital now! Can you call Henry Mayo Emergency Room and tell them that we're on the way?"

"Sir, do you need an ambulance or not?"

"No! I need you to call the hospital for me! My daughter is having a seizure!"

"Sir, I cannot do this. All I can do is call an ambulance."

The next seizure occurred after Vivien attended a friend's birthday party. A big inflatable "bouncy" was featured, a staple at many parties. After playing joyfully and vigorously for nearly four hours, she came home and went to sleep like always.

I don't know why but I woke up at five in the morning to check on Vivien. I had a feeling something was going to be wrong. As I leaned over Vivien she suddenly sat up and vomited on her sheets. This time I called the emergency room directly and told them we were on the way. Luckily the nurse remembered us. We ran past the front window and the nurse opened the door just as a security guard jumped up from behind a counter.

"Hey, you can't go in there!" he yelled.

"It's okay," said the nurse.

"No, they need identification!"

I handed Vivien off to Nicole and she ran down the hallway with the nurse. The hospital security guard grabbed my arm. I pushed him back. "Don't touch me!"

"You're under arrest!"

"For what?"

He pulled out a canister of pepper spray. "Assault on an officer!"

"You're not a cop, you're a security guard! Get outta my way!"

I snatched the canister out of his hand and threw it across the floor, ran into Vivien's room. She was convulsing.

Vivien needed two doses of Ativan. Her seizure stopped, but then started again after five minutes. When she finally woke up, she looked at me and said, "There's two of you, Daddy."

When we got back home, we placed her on the couch in the living room, because she didn't like her bedroom after a seizure. We covered the windows and turned off the lights; she always craved sleep after a seizure. I also placed a sign on the front door to deter solicitors, who seemed to bang on the door only when Vivien came home from the hospital.

There were many times when Vivien threw up and Nicole and I would stay up all night waiting for a seizure that never came. But it was always better to be tired than back in the hospital.

After a while it started to feel like Nicole and I knew more about the seizures than the doctors did. We devised some of our own empirical steps. Because all of Vivien's seizures happened after waking up early in the morning, Nicole and I decided to stop giving her naps during the day. And because her seizures always happened while or after she had a cold or flu, we monitored her closely if she got sick.

Over time, we developed a sixth sense for when a seizure might occur. No one else could sense it, because no one else had witnessed her seizures from beginning to end. Family and friends didn't know what to expect, because her seizures weren't like something you might see on television or in a movie. Her body didn't go full-tilt each time. She would start out slow. One moment she would be laughing and running around, and the next she'd pause, as if she was going into a trance. Her eyelids would flutter and her mouth would droop to the right. Then, her head would shift back up to the right. She would be awake, but unable to communicate. If we didn't give her the medication in time, she would fall unconscious.

I made a hospital kit, a book bag filled with all the necessary items for the next ER trip. I wrote everything down, because I knew I wouldn't remember anything.

We kept a list of all her medications and dosages, as the doctors rarely remembered what they'd prescribed. I kept a calendar, so that we knew the date of the last doctor visit and how much she had grown; her weight and height were vital to proper dosage. We made lists and gave them to family members in case of emergency. The refrigerator was covered with reminder notes, doctor appointment cards, and prescriptions.

I put copies of all of Vivien's medical records into a binder, including copies of her CT scan and MRI. I placed two fruit juice boxes in the front pocket of my hospital kit, because the hospitals never had any kid-friendly juices. I put ten dollars in the side pocket, for the valet parking service; the valet always took the car after we left it running on our way into the ER.

I packed extra clothes and toys in a plastic bag, along with a cell-phone charger. I kept the bag next to the front door, waiting for the next seizure to arrive.

I became a helicopter dad on steroids.

We arranged to visit a relative in Maryland for Thanksgiving, but Vivien had a panic attack on the way to the airport. Another curious thing we were discovering: her injury had affected much more in her brain than we could imagine. For instance, anything that was unfamiliar to Vivien seemed to cause a panic attack or seizure.

Aware that we were going to the airport—her very first time—Vivien was frozen in fear the entire ride. She seemed to relax as we got through the ticket gate, but then she began to panic once we stood in line to board the plane. We had prepped her months in advance, and she had seemed excited about traveling. But being at the airport was a different story. She grabbed Nicole by the hand and pulled her out of line.

"I want to go home, Mommy!" she cried.

It was too late. We had already paid for our tickets, and family was expecting us. I picked her up and carried her onto the plane. She kicked and screamed. The passengers on the plane whispered and stared. I began to panic myself, thinking about what was I going to do with my panicked child for a five-hour flight. I found our seats and set Vivien down, hoping a movie would relax her. I took out her portable DVD player, and put on her favorite cartoon. It didn't help. She continued to go berserk. A flight attendant came over and tossed me a package of cookies, as if it was a magic tonic.

Then a seizure began and I picked her up. Nicole grabbed our things, and we darted off the plane with her. The stewardess chased after us.

"You can't leave once you've boarded!"

"We're a little busy," I yelled.

I laid Vivien on the floor of the jet bridge. Nicole pulled the Diastat out of her purse, popped the cap, administered it to Vivien. The stewardess turned and closed the airplane door. A burst of air shot through the jet bridge as the plane departed. Minutes later the seizure stopped. We held Vivien and promised each other we'd never take her on a vacation again.

Vivien's next seizure was at one in the morning. When we got to the hospital, she was given Ativan, but her blood pressure and heart rate increased. One second she was fine, and the next she went into cardiac arrest.

She was resuscitated and rushed to Northridge Hospital, twenty miles away, into the pediatric neurology wing. Family and friends arrived, and Vivien seemed to make a recovery. I always had to keep in mind that she hated hospitals; she was never completely herself until she got home.

In the hospital room next to us was actor Greg Grunberg

from the TV show *Heroes*. His son, who also had epilepsy, had suffered a serious seizure. Greg founded TalkAboutIt. com to bring awareness of epilepsy. With any disease you feel like you're the only one living with it. It was comforting to know that others were going through the same experiences.

By the eighth seizure we made plans to move. We put our house on the market and looked for schools in Sierra Madre. We were going to move in with my mom so Nicole could quit her job and focus on Vivien.

Vivien was on 7.5 milliliters of Keppra twice a day. Even with that much medication, she was still having seizures. We had to lower the dosage because it left her in a zombie-like state, barely able to speak. She was a visibly different child.

We started to pack and put our things in boxes. Nicole and I were in survival mode. Our lives were spiraling out of control and we knew it. We also knew that moving in with my mom wouldn't solve our problems; it would only make certain things worse. Nicole knew that even though she wanted to stay home, going to work helped her cope with the situation. It's important to take up an outside interest to get your mind off of the disease and forget about the pain inside. Even if it means going to work.

We knew that breaking from the routine we already had would cause more stress. Vivien loved our home, and she was going to put up a fight if we moved. Vivien hated change. So we stayed.

I hated asking Vivien about the seizures but I wanted to know if she experienced any pain. After one of her now countless seizures, when we got home from the hospital, I asked her what she remembered.

"I died and went to heaven with God, but he told me that you and Mommy needed me more down here on earth," she said.

It seemed like such a normal response that I didn't ask any more questions. It just made sense. It made sense why God had never listened to me. He was too busy taking care of Vivien. Of course I was dumfounded, but I loved hearing her say these things. It lifted my spirit and gave me hope that one day we would end epilepsy. Vivien inspired me to be a better person and see life in a different way. I understood that attending to Vivien's needs gave my life purpose.

Nicole and I took turns sleeping in Vivien's room. I didn't want to miss a seizure. I had so much guilt for missing the first one that almost killed her. Everyone offered advice on why we shouldn't sleep in Vivien's room. They encouraged us to get a seizure dog instead.

Childrearing teaches us not to coddle a child. Break the bond early, so they can become independent. I tried for several nights to do this, but I kept getting up every ten minutes to check on Vivien. I wasn't going to let another seizure go undetected. When her brain activity was at its peak, she would wake up screaming from night terrors, and run down the hallway. So, it was simply easier to just sleep in her room, just in case. I also read online about a father who gave up sleeping in his six-year-old son's room because the child hadn't had a seizure in more than a year. Then one morning he went to check on him, and the boy was dead. I didn't want to be a dad who might have caught the seizure if only he'd slept in his child's room.

In the end Nicole and I were alone as parents. We

couldn't travel far from the hospital or leave Vivien alone at night. We were part-time prisoners in our own home. The Diastat medication stopped working and for awhile we had to rely on getting Vivien to the hospital because her seizures weren't stopping on their own. Her disorder was Status Epilepticus, a life-threatening condition in which the brain is in a state of persistent seizure. Our doctor mentioned the drug Midazolam, but it wasn't available as a rescue medication. It wasn't available at all. We would have to bypass the medical system in order to get it. We would have to administer it with a syringe in Vivien's arm. We liked the idea better than the rectal gel, but I had never used a syringe and it scared me. We had a nurse train us on how to use a syringe with the Midazolam. We were told we were the first parents to be trained with the drug. I was able to pay cash for the medication, and ordered a box of needles off the Internet.

The next seizure arrived just as the sun came up. Vivien sat up in bed and said that she felt sick. I carried her to the bathroom and she threw up. I turned on the lights. Her eyes were fluttering and she was shaking. I called for Nicole who was sleeping. She had agreed to give her the shot. I carried Vivien to the couch and laid her down. Nicole ran over with the syringe and a bottle of liquid Midazolam. She pulled off the cap to the needle and drew the liquid into the syringe.

"I can't do this," she said.

We were running out of time. The seizure always got worse the longer it went on.

I grabbed the syringe and plunged it into Vivien's arm.

She screamed. I pulled the needle out and held her. Nicole called 911, but by the time the ambulance arrived and we got to the hospital, the seizure had stopped. It was another small miracle. Within a few hours Vivien was back to normal. The new medication was far superior to the old. After four years of fighting epilepsy, we had finally won a small victory.

Chapter Nine

THERAPY

After Vivien's first seizure we were referred to occupational therapy twice a week. Vivien had lost some motor skills and needed to re-train her brain. In the brain, we learned, the two hemispheres communicate with each other to process information. They work together to formulate a single thought. Vivien's brain wasn't doing that. She was having problems with the right side of her body, and some trouble with her mobility. She was falling down a lot. The right side of her body was weak and her right leg sometimes gave out when she was running. Her right arm was also weak, and it was hard for her to hold things in her hand. Before the seizure, she'd been using her right hand to draw. After, she'd switched to her left hand.

The therapy focused on building her core muscles so that she could have the strength to rebuild her other muscles. The objective was to create a comfortable setting where her brain could respond properly to fear, change, or new information—all of which at this point would send her into a panic like the one on the plane.

In a way you could say that Vivien's occupational therapy helped legitimize her disease in our minds. She had it. Okay. We were ready to deal with it. We were ready to take the bull by the horns. Therapy was never suggested by the doctors; it was an outside option that Nicole and I chose based on our own research and intuition. And our need to do something besides wait for the next seizure to occur. According to our research, most parents did not consider it in similar cases. I figured we had to do everything we could. Everybody knows that in medicine today, you have to be creative; you have to be your own best idea person and your own best advocate.

We were told that Vivien would never be "normal," so I was in favor of doing therapy. In some ways, I will admit, I was hoping we could "fix" Vivien, put my beautiful baby back to where she deserved to be. What I didn't like about therapy was that I couldn't be in the room with her during the hour-long session. The reason was because most parents couldn't stop themselves from interrupting the child. Parents were a distraction. I was allowed to sit in the waiting room, which I did while the other parents dropped their kids off and left. The therapy gave me a way to gauge Vivien's disability. I would sit in the lobby waiting. Sometimes to pass the time I would look up rare diseases on my iPhone. I don't know why. I think it gave me a sense of the absolute randomness of the universe. Like they say, shit happens. Nobody is exempt.

Judging from some of the other children I saw, I felt like Vivien had a good chance of regaining her mobility. Some of the other children in therapy were visibly slow and required crutches or wheelchairs. Others had tics, such as barking or shouting. I saw the same group of parents weekly.

Billy's mother had been a crack addict. He blinked constantly. Carol had been struck by a car when she was seven while riding her bike. She failed to stop at a red light, and drove into traffic. Now she was severely mentally disabled.

In a way the therapy helped because it gave us a feeling of being active. It gave me something to track Viven's health. I could compare her to the other kids. As bad as it sounded, it gave me hope. Vivien seemed to be improving while the other children weren't.

Nicole had always obsessed about every part of Vivien's life, every developmental milestone. Vivien didn't crawl soon enough. Then she didn't walk soon enough. Vivien's hair didn't grow long enough. Her teeth hadn't come in. She wasn't potty-trained. I felt like therapy would ease Nicole's burden, if you know what I mean. And mine, too. There was someone with which to share the process, at least.

We shied away from social events. To a lot of parents, parenthood is a competition. At parties, parents tended to extoll the virtues of their offspring. Timmy could read by the age of two. Sally learned to tie her shoelaces at one year. Billy can write in Chinese and he's only six months old. Others would seem to try to pity us and offer us advice. What did they know about having an epileptic kid? I know they were trying to help, but it was difficult. I was

hurt and frustrated and just frickin' gut struck as it was—
and always trying to maintain for the sake of the family.
We all know how that goes. Maybe it was best if I didn't
integrate, if you know what I mean. If you're reading this
book, I'm sure you do.

Chapter Ten
LIKE THE WIND IN THE TREES

Before Vivien was born Nicole and I lived a block from my in-laws in Granada Hills. A neighborhood in the San Fernando Valley, twenty-five miles north of downtown Los Angeles, it had started out as a dairy farm and orchard known as Sunshine Ranch. The citrus groves were named after a city in Spain. In 1959 Soviet leader Nikita Khrushchev was taken to Granada Hills instead of Disneyland to tour an example of a typical, modern-day American neighborhood.

We rented a nice four-bedroom home from Nicole's parents, but they didn't understand boundaries. My father-in-law would walk into the house at all hours. I'd be coming out of the shower and he'd be standing in the bathroom.

"What are you doing?" he'd demand.

"I'm showering."

"You're wasting water?"

He didn't like the way I dressed, how I watered the lawn, or threw out the garbage. He had just retired and was stockpiling chickens, certain that the economy was going to collapse and we'd all be trading a basket of eggs for currency. I understood his side. I had taken his daughter and his second home. To keep our sanity, we moved out.

Even so, throughout this process, we wouldn't have been able to manage without our family. Even though I had my issues with my in-laws, we couldn't have managed Vivien's illness without them and our other close relatives. They were always there to lend their love and support as wonderful loving grandparents. Nicole's mother could always cheer up Vivien after a seizure. My mother was always there whenever we needed her and never complained. We, too, had our differences, but epilepsy made us a stronger family. I could always count on our family for help. It was something good that came out of all this, after a checkered family past.

We settled into a two-story condo just off the freeway in Canyon Country, with hardwood floors, shutters, and high ceilings. We painted and put in new carpet. We stayed for three years.

However, the moment we brought Vivien home, we knew we had outgrown the condo. We needed space and we needed safety. We didn't like the stairs; they were too steep. The third step from the bottom was a death trap; we both slipped and fell down holding the baby. Things that had always bothered us about the condo were now magnified. There was limited parking for guests, and strangers often parked in front of our garage door, blocking our exit. When the power went out in one part of the complex, it affected everyone. On more than one occasion we had to stay in a hotel, because it took days for the power to go back on. We packed up bags of breast milk and carried them to the hotel in an ice chest. I felt like an organ-donor courier.

Our neighbors were rude and the walls were paper-thin. We felt trapped. I heard every creak of my neighbors' homes.

Crime was also creeping around the block. The mini-market down the street was robbed three times in a month. Graffiti appeared on walls and street signs. The streets got louder. They felt more dangerous. We needed a safe place to raise our child. We needed a house with a backyard for the baby to play in without crazy neighbors banging on the walls or strangers trolling the neighborhood. The longer we stayed in the condo, the more I wanted to move into a new home. I obsessed about it.

When the baby was five months old, we decided to move.

I combed the Internet and drove to the homes and walked through the open houses. When I went house hunting, I could tell the short sales because the owners didn't bother to leave their homes, opting to sit on the couch watching TV in their underwear. They were trying to stay as long as they could until the bank sold their home.

I found a three-bedroom, two-bath home in northern Valencia, painted blue. The backyard was small, but with a hill that had a perfect area for a tree house. From the hill you could see Six Flags Magic Mountain theme park in the distance. The front yard was large, with lots of grass for Vivien to run around. Nicole and I named it Old Blue. This house spoke to me. It needed me just as much as I needed it. I drove the neighborhood at all hours to see whether it was a safe place to raise a child. I looked for all the things that annoyed me about the condo, but couldn't find them. We sold the condo for a loss and moved into the house in Valencia.

I didn't know it at the time but I was overwhelmed with work, the baby, and the expense of our new home. I measured everything by money, and the more we spent on our new home, the more I stressed. The hardwood floors were costing four times what I had estimated. We needed new electrical and windows. I was holding Vivien, then nine months old, when I was hit with a wave of intense fear. My heart was pounding and I felt dizzy. My vision was blurred. Everything I saw had a yellowish tint to it. Images were distorted, like I was intoxicated. I handed Nicole the baby and passed out.

At the hospital a doctor stood over me listening to my heartbeat.

"Have you been having any stress lately?" the doctor asked.

"I just bought a house."

He laughed. "I did that one time. It was a money pit. Remember your health is more important than a house."

I thought buying a home would solve all my problems. I was fixated on owning a home for my family. Looking back at that time, I felt like I was suffocating. The weight of the world seemed to be on me, but in reality it was just a home. I thought I needed a home to be happy. When epilepsy entered my life, I realized that when you change your needs, you change your perceptions. My life wasn't about fixing up a home; it was about fixing epilepsy. I had thought that a home would solve things. I had thought my life would be defined by major events, but in reality it was the little moments that I couldn't hold in my hand. What made me complete now was making Vivien's lunch, walking her to school, and listening to her first-grade problems.

One sunny Sunday afternoon we were driving to my niece's birthday party when we passed Henry Mayo Hospital. Vivien was in the backseat holding her pink bunny. It had been a year since her last seizure. A year since she had beaten death. Vivien was three. She pointed to the hospital.

"I remember that place, Mommy."

"What place?" asked Nicole, looking up from her iPhone.

"The hospital."

"What do you remember about it?"

"That's where I died and came back to life."

I looked at Nicole. Tears welled in her eyes.

"Did you go to heaven, honey?" I asked trying to joke. "Heaven should be radical. With rainbows and unicorns."

"I told them I wanted to stay here with you."

Nicole grabbed my hand and squeezed it. I glanced back in the mirror.

"You told who?"

"God."

"You met God, honey?"

"Yes. He was very nice."

I was struck with a wave of emotion. I pulled the car over, too shocked to drive. Then I turned back to look at Vivien. "Can you tell Daddy more about what happened?"

"God wrapped me in a warm blanket and told me I was going home with you. He said life is a puzzle and it is up to you to put the pieces together. He's like Mother Nature, Daddy. Like the wind in the trees."

Chapter Eleven

YOU GOTTA HAVE FAITH

Another year went by. Vivien turned six and we celebrated with a winter-themed birthday party at the ice rink. We lowered her medication. A few weeks passed, and we lowered her medication again. Her prognosis was good and it looked like she was going to have a normal life. Our goal was to get her off medication completely. The doctor finally said the words that I'd been waiting four years to hear: "I think she's going to be just fine."

Our good fortune was short-lived. Epilepsy had been stalking us the entire time. By lowering her medication, we invited epilepsy back into our lives. Vivien started school. It was our best opportunity to see whether Vivien was getting better. Mostly she had been around family, and relied on us. We wanted her to just be normal, but we might have skipped over things, blinded by our love and our desire to see her succeed. School would be the ultimate test. I wanted her to be treated just like everyone else, but I didn't want her to be bullied for her epilepsy. Nicole felt the same way. She had been bullied in school for being deaf, and being half-Mexican hadn't helped either where she'd grown up.

I had hated school. I had dyslexia and attention deficit disorder, and I was a poor student. I would watch my mother drive off and I would burst into tears standing in front of my school holding my NASA lunch box. My father had moved out for a while and was living on his sailboat. I saw him every other week. It didn't help that Sister Jean, who had a permanently dead arm in a sling, told me that I was going to hell because I wasn't really a Catholic. She told me in front of our class and scolded me for spelling my name wrong.

"You are the stupidest child I've ever had in my class," she said.

The other children laughed. It left a lasting impression on me. I never forgot that moment. When I told my parents, they agreed that I wasn't the sharpest pencil in the box. So I stopped using "Michael" and took "Mike" instead. It was easier to remember and harder to misspell.

Later my guidance counselor advised me to drop out of school when I was fourteen. I was shocked. I had been in high school only a few months.

I feared my genes wouldn't help Vivien much in the intelligence department. I might not have been able to read or write, but at least I was going to make sure that Vivien had my full support. I was trying to change my childhood tragedies into triumphs.

In February her class had a Valentine's Day assembly for parents and family members. I stood at the back of the crowded school auditorium, video-recording the children as they walked up on stage. I wasn't sure how Vivien was going to take being in front of such a large crowd. My fear was that she was going to freeze up and forget her lines. She had always been so shy around people, and I wasn't sure if she would remember all the words to the Nat King Cole song "L-O-V-E." When the music started, I couldn't believe my eyes. I was dead wrong. She sang and danced her heart out, leading the other children standing on the bleachers. I had feared that she would struggle keeping up with children her age, and here she was leading them all.

"L is for the way you look at me! O is for the only one I see! V is very, very extraordinary! E is even more than anyone that you adore, and love is all that I can give you!"

At that moment, I knew everything was going to be okay. There would always be trials and torments and things I couldn't control. Fatherhood under the best of circumstances is a trial. And sure, I'd like to think there would be no more seizures, but I'm not going to go there.

A sudden calm swept over me. For the first time in years, I felt at peace. I knew my place. I knew what I was here for—to be Vivien's father. I believe with all my heart that Vivien was sent to me to strengthen my faith and bring us closer together as a family.

One evening as we lay in bed watching TV, Nicole said to me, "I don't believe in God. Is that bad?" Vivien was asleep in her room. She had just come back from the hospital after suffering another seizure. I checked on her every few minutes with the baby camera monitor.

"I don't think it's bad if it's how you feel," I told her.

In my mind, I wasn't really sure about God either. Every time Vivien had a seizure, I'd prayed for them to stop. Of course, my prayers did nothing to stop the seizures. And bigger than that, how could one religion be better than another? How could so many people be allowed on this earth and only a special few be allowed in heaven?

Nicole had always been more religious than me. She had been raised a good Catholic girl, filled with guilt, doubt, and remorse. She told me one time that she was a believer because she survived a serious explosion. In 1994 the Northridge earthquake rocked Southern California. Nicole and her family ran outside of their house just as the sky filled with a mushroom cloud of black smoke. The earthquake had broken the city's main gas line and caused dozens of homes to explode, killing several families.

Nicole had faith when we first met, but now she had lost it. At one time, she kind of looked down on me for not seeking out God. I was more of the nonbeliever. I just went along for the ride to please her. It was different now. She had come over more to my skeptical way of thinking. Both of us were looking for answers to our daughter's disease.

Nicole turned off the TV. "Why did this have to happen to us?"

"I don't know. I wish I did. But if anyone can handle it, it's you and me."

The morning of her first major seizure, when Vivien

died and came back to life, there were only a handful of people in the room. Skeptics will say that she never really was in danger, because she was in a hospital. They will say she survived by chance and science and skill.

But after Vivien's first seizure, something changed in me. I started to believe... in something. I don't know why. I can't explain my thinking. It's irrational, not logical at all. It's just a feeling I have. The truth was, I felt that He had held up His end of the bargain I asked for when I prayed for Vivien to return to us alive. I felt I should return the favor by being a better person. Maybe like Vivien said, "God is the wind in the trees."

We can't see love, but we can feel it. Love drives people insane. Love is real. We invest in it. We can't see sorrow either, but it goes hand and hand with love. Maybe God is all those feelings and emotions. I wasn't sure of God. I was afraid. I was afraid of what I didn't know and couldn't see. Maybe God is science and naturalism combined. Maybe God knows that we are connected when we are preoccupied with the needs of others.

Epilepsy allowed me a new reality. I knew something; I just didn't know what. I knew that the past dictated the future. I knew that if I held onto a negative past, my future would be negative, and so would Vivien's.

I used to think that belief in God was a crutch, but now I look to God for inspiration. It comforts me knowing that someone might be watching out for me.

I was never any good at math; it was by far my worst subject. But in order to graduate from college, I had to take math. So I studied hard, and I flunked the first semester. I repeated the course, and flunked it again. On my third try I got an "A." To this day I have no idea how I got that grade. I did question it, but then I forgot about it. I like to think of God as a math problem, an equation that I will never understand. Did God come to Vivien's rescue? I don't know, but I like to think he did. Medicine is not always an exact science. It is trial and error. So, why can't faith in God be trial and error?

I have no concrete answers right now, but I have faith in the journey. I have faith that the outcome will be good. You've got to have faith in something, or life does not get better. It remains stagnant.

Vivien died and came back to us forever changed, and because of this I went through all the stages of grief. I was angry. I was shocked that Vivien had been so healthy one day and in the throes of a horrible disease the next. I was in denial that the seizures would come back. I was angry that this was happening to my family. I tried to find a reason. I felt guilty that I could not control it. I sank into a depression. Sometimes life becomes so unbearable with a sick child that you just want to give up but you can't. Then I started to look within myself. I started to accept the things I could not change, and work for a better life for Vivien. It was up to me to give her the best life possible.

Maybe God was reaching out to me through my daughter. Maybe there was a reason for all of this. It's up to me to figure it out. What's important is to use life's trials and tragedies to your advantage, because these uncontrollable events remind us to stay focused on what's really important.

In the end, it's your faith in something better that keeps you going.

Chapter Twelve

NEW
SCHOOL

The best way to tell if Vivien was improving was to have her interact with other people. It was important to get her out of the normal routine and challenge her brain. I couldn't keep her at home for the rest of her life even though I wanted to.

I tried to hold back the tears on the first day of school but it was difficult. I was afraid of letting go even though the school was close to home. There were two teachers in a class of twenty kids. The teachers were both mothers. Nicole and I sat down with them and discussed Vivien's epilepsy. They didn't mind keeping Vivien's medications in the classroom cupboard. They were eager to learn about epilepsy so I felt comfortable leaving Vivien there. Vivien's seizures had taken on a pattern. They usually occurred right after she woke up, so I waited around at her school every morning to make sure she was okay. She rarely had a seizure after nine in the morning. If I waited around until nine I had better peace of mind for the rest of the day. We made sure to tell her teachers not to let her nap at school.

Some mornings Vivien didn't look right so I kept her home. It was hard to detect the seizures but she always had a glassy look to her eyes a few minutes before a seizure. I waited in her classroom until I felt comfortable leaving Vivien alone. Some mornings I stayed for several hours. The teachers were more than happy to have me volunteer and they put me to work.

I made copies for the kids' homework or put together crafts for upcoming projects. I made twenty pumpkins out of orange paper for Halloween and twenty more turkeys out of brown paper for Thanksgiving. For Christmas I decorated the entire classroom and made cupcakes. I was always cutting, pasting, and making copies for Vivien's class. I walked Vivien to class every morning, holding her hand along the way and praying she wouldn't have a seizure. I prayed she wouldn't struggle like I did in school. I prayed a lot because I didn't have any hope that her epilepsy would ever get better.

One morning I walked past a guy I had grown up with in Pasadena. It had been twenty years but I recognized him instantly. He had been my best friend in first grade. We shared the same name and birthday. We had several double birthday parties and used to ride our bikes around Pasadena for hours. He was the only kid I ever knew who had news radio come out of his mouth. The radio had played through his braces in fourth grade. It was mind-blowing. We had been on the same soccer team four years in a row. His mother and my mother had been good friends. He had three daughters now and one of them was in Vivien's class. It was one of those moments where you think life is trying to whisper something to you. I thought it might be a sign. What were the odds that we would reconnect after all this time? He lived a block away from the school. He still had the same goofy smile like he had when we were twelve.

"Mike!" I called out.

"Do I know you?" he asked, with a puzzled look.

"It's Mike Knox. I haven't seen you in twenty years."

"No, I just saw you on social media the other day."

"But you never said anything? I haven't seen you in person in twenty years."

He wasn't excited to see me. He wasn't excited at all. He acted like we were strangers. If he had seen me on social media he would have known about Vivien's epilepsy. He never said anything. I said hello to him for the next couple of weeks but it didn't seem like he wanted to see me. One day we just stopped saying hello and faded into a crowd of parents. One of the hardest pills to swallow was realizing that family and friends knew about Vivien's epilepsy but never asked about her. It was something that took me years to get over. Some people just handled situations differently. Some people didn't care, but most just didn't know how to respond. It was easier to ignore things. I couldn't get upset when they didn't care. It was weird getting old. The people I thought I knew best. I finally understood why people home-schooled.

Vivien excelled in school. Even though it was just

nursery school we were excited for her future. She was doing all the tasks the school asked. She was interacting with the other kids and making friends. She learned to be fair and didn't get upset when someone didn't want to share. She was hitting all her milestones. She had taken a major step into higher education and come out on the other side unscathed. The year flew by and before I knew it Vivien had graduated to kindergarten.

Kindergarten started at 7:45 instead of 9 a.m. It was a bigger world now. Vivien was taking on more responsibilities. The school began to present challenges to me as a parent. I wasn't allowed to be late every day like nursery school. We had entered the big leagues and the old rules didn't apply. Instead of dealing with two nursery school teachers that used baby talk, I was up against the adult teachers now. Everyone had their place of power, from the principal down to the yard duty staff. Now that Vivien was in kindergarten I wasn't allowed to walk her to class.

The school didn't want the parents on campus after 8 a.m. The nursery school had been right next to the street and parents were allowed to park in the school parking lot. It had only been a few feet to the classroom door. Dropping Vivien off at school had been stress-free. The nursery school playground had been fenced off from the upper grades and felt secure. Now all the grades were together, mingling like a prison yard. The kindergarten kids walked in with the older kids. Even though the kindergarten classroom was in the front of the school the kids entered through the back. They walked past the front doors, which were locked for security reasons, and around to the back of the school.

Parents had to park two blocks from the school and walk around the corner to the crossing guard. I was jockeying for a parking spot like I was at the mall. It was a rush to the far end of the school. If we didn't make it to the gate at 7:45 the yard duty staff would lock the gate. Parents would have to walk back around to the front of the school and get a late pass from the front desk. I pleaded my case to the principal but he didn't care. He was heartless when it came to any child with a disability. He reminded me of a short and swollen Ricky Schroder. He was planning to run for the school board and couldn't be bothered with parent problems.

"I think you're being a bit of a mama bear," he chuckled one morning behind his office desk.

"All I'm asking is that I can walk my daughter to class," I pleaded. "She has epilepsy."

"We have yard staff that can walk her to class."

"Do your yard staff even know what a seizure is? You can't walk someone to class that's having a seizure. Her seizures are life threatening. What happens if no one is there?"

"I can assure you every morning I will have someone there to watch her. I really think you're just being overly dramatic."

I questioned myself. Had I become too paranoid? Maybe I needed to let Vivien grow a little on her own? Maybe I needed to let go as a parent. I was always doubting myself.

"I'll try it your way," I said reluctantly.

"Trust me. Tomorrow morning Helga will greet you at the gate and then radio me over the school walkie-talkie that she's escorting your daughter to her class. Helga is from Sweden. Sweden has a superior education system to the United States. She's very good with kids."

He made it sound so easy that I almost believed him.

The next morning Helga wasn't at the gate. No one was at the gate. The principal wasn't there either. He had taken a sabbatical to the east coast. Helga had a mental breakdown and returned to Sweden.

The gate was locked before 7:45 and there were a group of parents cursing Principal "Little Ricky Schroder." I noticed that at the far end of the playground another gate opened to a public park behind the school. I complained to the school about the park but they weren't bothered by the fact that strangers could access the school. The reason for walking to the back of the school was so that strangers couldn't get on school grounds from the front of the school.

After that I walked Vivien through the front of the school each day into her class. The school wasn't happy about me going rogue. I had to be my child's advocate. This meant signing in each day that Vivien was late since she wasn't standing in line with the rest of her class at the back of the campus. Her teacher was less concerned about Vivien than the principal. If a child wasn't in her line at the back of the school they were marked down as absent. She didn't report them as late, but absent for the entire day. I thought it was a little extreme. She was an old German lady in her late sixties who used to be a Catholic nun. She left the convent under mysterious circumstances. She carried the wrinkles of a loveless woman. I don't think she had ever smiled in her entire life. She was strict and reminded me of my fifth grade teacher. Some of the other kids had nicknamed her Mrs. Snot Rocket. I thought it was a fitting name.

"Back in my day they would hit us with a twitch if we got out of line," Mrs. Snot Rocket expressed to me one morning. "My style of teaching has helped me survive for 38 years in this hell."

I wanted to tell her it was time to hang it up and retire.

"I was hoping you'd make an exception for my daughter. She has epilepsy and it's difficult for her to be in stressful environments."

"Stress can be good for children. It builds character."

"Stress causes her to have seizures."

Mrs. Snot Rocket objected. "No exceptions to being late."

"She keeps getting marked down as absent when she's just late. We're going to be late every morning until she no longer has seizures."

"Life is difficult Mr. Knox and I don't make exceptions for anyone. If we had made exceptions we would have lost World War II. If I make exceptions for you I have to make exceptions for everyone."

"I'm pretty sure I'm the only one asking. If Vivien keeps getting marked down as absent then it looks like I'm not taking her to school. I look like a bad parent."

"Maybe you are a bad parent if you can't bring your child to school on time. Maybe if Vivien applied herself a little more she could get herself here on time."

"It's not that simple. She has a brain injury so she doesn't think the same way that you and I think. I mean, she's just a child. She knows what a car is but if I handed her the keys she doesn't know how to drive the car. We can't expect her to think like an adult."

"There's no better time to grow up than now."

I gave up trying to talk to Mrs. Snot Rocket and Principal Little Ricky Schroder. My next battle was with Diane who worked at the front desk. She looked like someone with a hundred dead cats back at her apartment. I named her the Crazy Cat Lady. She had a thousand-yard stare reserved for mental patients on Thorazine. Every day she wore the same green knitted sweater that was coated in a thick layer of cat fur. I was supposed to get a late pass and a visitor pass at the front desk from Diane. There was always a long line so I would take Vivien to her class first and then sign in later. I was the only parent that walked their child inside the school and the only one at the front desk.

Diane was usually preoccupied with selling raffle tickets or some other fundraiser for the school. I tried to make friends with the Cat Lady because I wanted her to remember Vivien in case she had a seizure at school. The Cat Lady always looked at me blankly and asked what I was doing at the school. The first few weeks I tried to remain calm and repeated that I was walking my daughter to class because she had epilepsy.

"You can't come into the front," screamed the Cat Lady. "You have to walk her to the back of the school!" She repeated this to me each morning like a broken record.

"I know but my daughter is already in her classroom. I just need a visitor pass."

"Why do you want a visitor pass?" Cat Lady Demanded.

"My daughter has seizures so I want to watch her until I'm comfortable with leaving."

"Parents aren't allowed in the classroom."

"I know but I can watch from the hallway through the windows. They're very large."

"Have you talked to the principal about this?"

"He has been very helpful," I lied. "He told me it's not a problem."

To bypass Cat Lady I made my own visitor pass and attached it to a plastic badge. No one bothered me after that because I had a badge.

A few weeks later I got a letter in the mail that I needed to appear in front of the school board for excessive absences. Mrs. Snot Rocket had reported me to the authorities. I wasn't the only parent there. Mrs. Snot Rocket had reported a dozen parents to the school board.

It was only fitting that the school board was late to a hearing about being late. I pleaded my case and the school board let me off with a warning. I knew I couldn't continue to break the rules. Somewhere along the line the school would get its revenge. I wasn't going to make it to school on time. I wasn't even going to try. Making sure Vivien didn't have seizures was all I cared about.

The school union was having issues and didn't want to carry Vivien's rescue medication. I understood that the teachers didn't want the responsibility of giving medication, even though both teachers the previous year had no problem with it. The school union didn't want non-medical people saving children's lives without getting paid. I thought it was absurd the school nurse couldn't put it in the cabinet next to the Epipens approved for children who were allergic to peanuts.

Principal Little Ricky Schroder came up with a plan.

"We will just call 911 in case Vivien has a seizure at school and then the hospital will call to inform you that she's at the hospital."

It seemed to me it would be easier if the school nurse could give Vivien the rescue medication before the ambulance arrived. It would save a lot of time and probably her life.

A month went by and after six meetings with Little Ricky Schroder I decided to contact an attorney. I felt exhausted trying to do what was right. I didn't want to hire an attorney but my hands were tied. It took a dozen phone calls but I finally found an attorney that agreed to meet with me. I wasn't looking to sue the school. I just wanted the school to do their job.

One phone call from an attorney and the school was more than happy to have Vivien's medication on campus. After that, I stopped talking to Principal Little Ricky Schoder and had the attorney mediate for me. Everything moved quickly with the attorney. It was sad but the reality was that no one was going to help us without the threat of a lawsuit. Having an attorney seemed to open doors that had never been there before. I knew the school would fight back. It was like going up against the government. I just wanted the peace of mind that Vivien's rescue medication would be there if she had a seizure. I wasn't confident that anyone at the school would use it but maybe I'd be there if it happened.

After the attorney called about the rescue medication Vivien's demeanor changed. She was no longer the happy child that loved school. She was afraid of Mrs. Snot Rocket, Little Ricky Schroder and the Crazy Cat Lady. I was certain the school wanted payback. I couldn't prove it but Vivien wasn't being treated the same way she was before.

Vivien had always struggled but she had done it with determination. Now she was giving up. She didn't have the courage to fight back against adults. She had trouble falling asleep at night. During the night she was pulling at her hair and grinding her teeth. She woke up complaining of a headache or stomach ache; insisting she was too sick to go to school. I waited around in the morning longer and longer. She didn't want me to leave her alone anymore.

No matter what we tried to do the fact remained that she hated going to school. I wanted the school to have sympathy for Vivien. The school had won several awards when they first opened. They displayed large banners on the front of the school but they were ten years old now. Principal Little Ricky Schroder was so proud of his old awards.

"Can you just give Vivien a break because of her disability?" I pleaded.

"I don't deal with disabilities," he scoffed. "I deal with winners."

The attorney suggested setting up an IEP. Nicole called every member of the school board and a few members of the state assembly. We both felt defeated by the lack of effort the school was putting forth. The school had never mentioned an IEP. It stood for Individualized Education Program. It was a plan developed for each child with special needs in a public school. It was created with a team of educators and reviewed during the year. The IEP was a legal document spelling out Vivien's learning needs and the services the school would provide. Our lawyer felt it might finally hold the school responsible.

Vivien's seizures increased and I knew it was because of her school. The stress of hurrying to class after another sleepless night and then getting screamed at by her teachers had taken a toll on her health. We had tried our best to work with the school but it was time to look for a new school. Nicole found a charter school that was fifteen minutes away. I wasn't happy about the longer drive but I liked what the school had to offer.

Vivien sat in on a class for half a day and came home smiling. It was the happiest I had seen her in months. Her epilepsy had always made her afraid of change but she was so miserable at her school that she craved the change. It was a huge step for her choosing to go to a new school. There was no homework and no tests. Vivien wouldn't have the pressure of studying for an exam. She wouldn't have to come to school after a seizure and be surprised by a pop quiz. Her memory was bad enough, even when she wasn't surprised with a test from Mrs. Snot Rocket.

The school wanted the parents to be involved. I could sit in class all day if I wanted to. The new school didn't mind that I brought Vivien late every morning. Vivien's new class didn't start until 8:45 a.m., which meant Vivien could sleep in later. They understood that her seizures were in her sleep and she would make a better student when she wasn't tired. The school nurse took all of our seizure medications with no questions asked and didn't require me to sign any paperwork.

Since it was halfway through the school year we had to wait until Vivien was accepted in the charter school. It was another long week at the old school but we promised

Vivien every day that she wouldn't ever have to see the Crazy Cat Lady, Mrs. Snot Rocket, and Little Ricky Schroder.

While we waited for the new school we had our first meeting with the IEP team. I always felt a need to talk to anyone that would listen about epilepsy. There was such a stigma. Movies and TV shows were still making fun of seizures. No one seemed to realize it wasn't a joke. Children were still getting bullied in school for seizures.

Every year Nicole and I had to sit down with Vivien's class and make them understand that seizures were serious. People with epilepsy didn't want to talk about it. They were hiding it from their spouses and partners. They didn't want their families to know because they were embarrassed. It was the fourth most common neurological disorder, with more than 3.4 million people affected in America. More people were dying from seizures than breast cancer. 50,000 people died each year in the United States and no one was talking about it. I saw so much pain with epilepsy. There were so many needless deaths. I never got upset with Vivien if she woke me up early or kept me up late. I knew there were a million other fathers that dreamed of having just one more second with their child.

Nicole and I met half a dozen school officials. All of them specialized in something that was going to fix Vivien. The only problem was not one of them specialized in epilepsy. There was a woman in a purple dress and matching hat who specialized in speech therapy.

"I think she has a speech impediment. We should start her on speech therapy right away."

There was a man with a long gray ponytail that specialized in fine motor skills.

"Your daughter has flat feet. Her seizures could be cured with the right shoes. I can make the molds in the back of my van."

A husband and wife team specialized in marriage and family therapy.

"We promise to fix your marriage. Her seizures are most likely caused by your marriage problems. We wrote a book on this very subject!"

Another young woman with a nose ring suggested that we use massage therapy.

"I will rid your daughter of the evil toxins that are ravishing her body."

Mrs. Snot Rocket had made it clear to the room that Vivien was failing her class. I knew she wasn't. I had kept her test scores and brought them with me to our meeting. I didn't care if Vivien failed out of school because her health was more important to me than her grades.

Principal Little Ricky Schroder chimed in, "Vivien's grades could bring down all the other kids' averages. If she just tried harder the entire school could bring up their averages and we might win another award!"

"In all my years I've never had a child fail my class," insisted Mrs. Snot Rocket.

"She's not failing your class," I replied.

"I just gave the students a quiz on Monday and she got a 57%."

"She also got a 90% on the test you gave her two weeks ago. She had a seizure the night before. I don't think it's fair that she has to take a test after having a seizure when she loses all of her memory."

"Life isn't fair. According to my calculations she's failing the class."

"I'm no math genius but I have her tests and her average is an 83%. I got through college with a 70%. That's a 'C' average."

"That's failing in my book," Mrs. Snot Rocket cackled.

"Maybe some speech therapy might help," insisted the lady in the purple dress.

I looked over at Nicole who was about to lose it. Her phone vibrated. She checked her text messages. There was a message from the charter school telling us that Vivien had been accepted to her new school. Nicole grabbed my hand.

The room erupted into an argument over Vivien's future. Nicole and I walked out. No one seemed to notice we were gone. We hurried home to tell Vivien the good news.

Chapter Thirteen
MY OFFICE STALKER

When I looked up from Vivien's hospital bed two hours had passed. My cell phone rang. I stepped out of the hospital room to answer it. My boss, Glenn, was looking for me. I was late for work. I tried to keep it together. My voice cracked. I could see my bottom lip trembling. I struggled to find the right words.

"Where the fuck are you?!" Glenn demanded.

"I'm in the hospital. My daughter flat-lined. I don't know what's going on but I can't come to work today."

"Why not?!" Glenn screamed.

"I'm in the hospital with my daughter. I don't know if she's going to live."

"What reports do you have due today?" Glenn asked.

"I don't know. I can't think right now."

"You better get your head out of your ass if you want to keep your job!"

It felt like Glenn was punching me in the face. I had expected him to understand. I wanted to hear some kind of empathy but Glenn was cold. His voice was distant. I wanted to lash out but I was numb. How could any human being be so heartless when told a child was in the hospital?

"Well, when are you coming to work?" Glenn scoffed.

"I don't know," I repeated.

"It's a simple question. Is it a day or a week?"

"I'm going to hang up now."

Nicole grabbed my phone and hung up for me. She turned the phone off and put it in her purse. She knew I needed to be rescued. We went back in the room and held Vivien's hand.

I would have stayed home from work longer but Glenn continued to call demanding to know when I was coming back to work. After three days of harassing phone calls I went to the office hoping to resolve things.

It was a long drive back to work. I didn't want to leave Vivien. I wanted to quit my job and stay home. Nicole and I talked about selling our home and moving in with my mom. We were in panic mode. We were preparing for the worst. I was furious that I had to leave my family to explain why I wasn't at work.

I entered the back door of my office and got halfway down the hallway when Glenn stopped me. He smiled and handed me a card. I thought the card was for me, but when I opened it, I saw it was for the janitor.

"Larry sprained his ankle," said Glenn. "So we got him

a get well card and a gift card. Everyone is chipping in five bucks."

"How did that happen?" I asked.

Glenn handed me a pen. I blindly signed the card and handed it back.

"The dumbass was roller skating," laughed Glenn.

"I'm glad he's okay."

"So, I heard you went to Vegas?" said Glenn.

"Who told you that?" I asked.

"You did. You said you really liked to gamble."

"I wasn't in Las Vegas. I was in the hospital with my daughter."

"Bummer. I love Vegas man. One time I won a bunch of money on the blackjack table and got two strippers. Best time of my life!"

"You know my daughter's sick. The only reason I came into work today was to speak to you about the way you've been treating me."

"This is news to me," said Glenn. "I thought you were on vacation."

"You know damn well I wasn't on vacation."

"Jesus, calm down. You don't have to flip out on me like you're having a seizure."

I didn't bother arguing. I knew he would never understand. I thought we could resolve everything with a handshake but it was obvious he was a psycho.

I left Glenn and went to Human Resources. I turned in a family leave form and went home to Vivien. The doctors didn't know what was wrong with her. She needed more tests. All I could do was wait by her side.

I took the next few weeks off. When it looked like

Vivien was going to be okay I came back to work. I had to return. I was running out of sick days. It was hard for me to be at home if I didn't need to be. My work was my identity.

When I got back to the office Glenn was waiting for me. He was waiting to retaliate against me for taking time off. He never asked how Vivien was or about my family. He focused on making my work life miserable. He turned everyone in the office against me. I expected them to understand but they treated me like I was a burden. The idea of having a sick child seemed to scare them. They didn't know what to say. No one asked how I was doing or how my family was doing. No one gave me a sympathy card or chipped in five dollars. There was no fundraiser at the office for epilepsy. They knew I had been absent from the office but never asked why. It was just easier to ignore the situation. They didn't have a problem telling me I looked overweight or old. I was going through hell and having to act like everything was normal at work.

I had known some of my coworkers for more than ten years. We had worked in a prison together. I thought we had bonded. I tried to talk to my coworkers about Glenn but it was difficult. They were afraid. Everyone had a story about how Glenn had wronged them. They all said he was a bully but no one wanted to stand up to him. It was the unspoken word that we took the abuse because it was part of the job. Gossip was the poor man's entertainment at my office. Glenn was a supervisor. He had all the power and no one dared to challenge him. Most of my coworkers wanted something from Glenn. They knew Glenn had contacts and he might help them get a promoted. After all we lived in Los Angeles, where people thrived by the motto "what can you do for me?"

As my boss, Glen was able to push the boundaries and dump more work on me. He moved my office to a windowless room and took away my company car. He submitted me to weekly drug tests. He monitored when I used the restroom. He went through my desk and checked my filing cabinet daily. He checked my phone messages and emails. He took down all the personal items I had put up.

"I moved your office so you'd be more comfortable," said Glenn. "It has better Wi-Fi. Also, you can't have pictures of your family on your desk. It's not work-related."

Every day was an interrogation about my work. He micromanaged everything I did. He followed me wherever I went. I tried to keep the peace. I was trying to keep my job. I needed the income in case something happened to Vivien. I needed health insurance. I tried my hardest not to react to Glenn because I knew that's what he wanted. However, I needed to protect myself and put Glenn on paper. I needed to document his abuse. I didn't want to file on Glenn but I felt I had to. The only way to protect myself was to put his name on paper first.

I went to file on Glenn but it was easier said than done. I had union rights but I had to fight for them. Glenn's supervisor told me to go to the head of the department. The head of the department told me to go to the union. The union told me to go to the office of the inspector general. No one wanted to help me.

"What do you want me to do," said Glenn's supervisor. "You need to get along or get it on."

"So, it's perfectly legal for a supervisor to harass an

employee?" I asked.

"Glenn is a super good guy," said the union president, putting his feet up on his desk. We went to high school together. He's one hell of a second baseman in our softball league."

It killed me that I was forced to pay union dues and they did nothing.

I went to the inspector general's office but the staff left me waiting in the lobby and went to lunch. I left after waiting a few hours. My phone calls and emails were ignored.

When Glenn found out he was furious. He intensified his stalking. I had poked the sleeping bear.

Glenn stalked me at work and then at home. The phone calls increased: hundreds of hang-ups from blocked numbers to my cell phone and home number. I started to notice things were out of place at my home.

First it was a flat tire. Then I found a plastic rat duct-taped to my front door. There was a bullet in my mailbox. My mail would be missing. Things in my house would be out of place. I couldn't be sure but it felt like someone had been in the house.

I put up video cameras hoping I could catch someone but never did. I was afraid for my family. I slept with a gun close to my bed. Not because of the thousands of felons I supervised but because I was afraid of my boss breaking into my house.

One morning I caught Glenn going through my trash-cans by the curb. He was holding my wife's cell phone bill.

"What are you doing?" I demanded.

Glen looked up from the garbage like a wild animal and

gave me a goofy smile.

"I was wondering if you were coming to work today?"

"You have my schedule. You know what time I'm coming to work."

"Oh, I wasn't sure."

"You could have called me on the phone."

"I forgot your phone number."

"What are you doing at my house?" I demanded.

"I'm trying to help you, Mike."

"You need help. I suggest you get back in your car and leave before I call the police."

I was in the gray area of the law. I couldn't call the police for my boss going through my trash. I wanted to get a restraining order but I couldn't prove that my boss was threatening my life. There wasn't a law against Glenn being creepy.

The next day Glenn called my mother at her home. He told her I was missing. It was the same day she had come home from the hospital. She was battling breast cancer and I had picked her up at the hospital after her surgery. I had taken the day off and Glenn knew where I was. I was out getting my mother's medication when he called. My mother feared the worse and called the police thinking I had been in a car accident. She wasn't exactly in the right state of mind that day.

It was one thing to bully me but when he reached out to my mother it made me furious. I sealed my fate when I filed on Glenn. There was no way the Department was ever going to promote me or do anything to help me. They were going to do everything to protect Glenn. I had nothing to lose by contacting an attorney.

I just wanted the harassment to end. I needed legal representation outside of the Department. Someone that had my best interests in mind and not the Department's. I was able to find an attorney through a coworker who had quit a year earlier because of stress.

"Get ready for all hell to break loose," the attorney joked.

Within a day of the attorney sending a letter to the Department I was bombarded with phone calls and emails. Managers and supervisors I had never met dropped by my office to plead Glenn's innocence.

"Glenn is just stressed from his divorce," said his supervisor.

"Glenn is a Christian," insisted a co-worker. He follows the word of the Lord. You wouldn't understand because you're not a religious person."

The attorney's letter scared Glenn and he pulled back on stalking me. He was trying to promote and any written allegations stopped him from promoting. Even though I was alienated at work the attorney had helped give me some power. Glenn stopped following me but then the Department started.

It was sad that everyone had a family and most of my coworkers had children. However, work always came first over family. Employment was a huge part of life. It made up our identity as adults. It was how we gauged our self worth. I wanted to be liked at work. I was a people pleaser. It always clouded my judgment. Being liked was also an important part of our existence. I wanted to be liked by my boss but he let me down. I just couldn't allow him to keep me down.

Not only had I sabotaged myself by being a whistle

blower, I had put my name on the Department's radar. I was now a snitch. The worst label a person could have in my line of work. I had crossed the line in law enforcement. The Department was going to go out of its way to discipline me.

A few days later I got a call from Agent Jones from Head-Quarters. I knew Jones. We had gone through the academy together. HeadQuarters didn't call to ask how you were doing. My name had been thrown in the hat. It was the quickest way to agitate someone in the Department. Just put a bug in their ear and start an investigation. Even if they didn't find anything tangible there was still a paper trail to drag your name through the mud.

Agent Jones asked me to meet him in Highland Park at 5 a.m. to do surveillance on one of my gang members. I hated leaving Vivien before 8 a.m. because there was always a chance she was going to have a seizure when I was gone.

I met up with Agent Jones in a gas station parking lot. It was after New Year's and the morning air was cold. Nearby homes were still lit up with Christmas lights and decorations.

Jones was a friend of mine but I knew I couldn't trust anyone. I was immediately suspicious that he was by himself.

"Where's the rest of your crew?" I asked.

"They're up the street."

They were filming me from another vehicle. I checked my rear view mirror but couldn't see anyone.

"How's everything going?" Jones asked.

"Not good," I said. "I've got Glenn all over me. He's trying to get me fired."

"I heard. He's a powerful guy. I would watch yourself."

"Easy for you to say," I said.

Jones already knew about my problems, which told me I was right. Jones turned on the car radio. He flipped the stations until he came to a Spanish station. He turned up the sound. He opened his jacket and pointed to a tiny microphone, pressing his index finger to his lips. He was telling me that he was wired and to be careful of what I said. I was already paranoid and now I was certain I was going to get fired.

"So what do you want me to do now?" I asked.

"Just be yourself. I'm going to act like a new agent and you show me around the parolee's house. I want to get a lay out before we go in and arrest him."

It all sounded like a set up to me. Jones didn't need my help. HeadQuarters never asked for help. I had been in the Department long enough to know that if they asked for help you were screwed.

I kept quiet knowing that everything was being recorded. I went through the motions and did everything Jones had told me to do. We were in and out of the house in ten minutes. I got lucky and nothing went wrong. The parolee was home and he didn't give me any problems. He wasn't smoking crack or loading a weapon on the coffee table. There were no psycho relatives snorting lines of cocaine off a broken toilet seat.

I dropped Jones off at the gas station and never saw him again. The events of that morning ate away at me. They were trying to make me look crazy. They wanted me gone.

I was a cornered animal they were trying to smoke out.

On the drive home I didn't feel well. My heart was pounding. I pulled over and vomited. I was sweating. I felt like I was having a heart attack. I pulled up to a store and bought some aspirin and water.

"Are you okay?" the cashier asked.

Her question only added to my paranoia. Of course a teenaged cashier with a shaved head and a nose ring could see that I was dying inside.

"I think so."

"You look stressed."

I knew I was stressed. That was an understatement. Stress was all I had known for years. My coworkers were just as bad. I was amazed we didn't shoot one another at the office from being stressed. The only good thing about being stressed was I craved sleep. It was my only escape. I crashed hard that night. It was a deep uninterrupted sleep.

I dreamed that I caught a mouse in the fireplace. I put the mouse in a plastic bottle and tossed it onto the front porch. Normally, I didn't remember dreams but this one stuck with me. It stayed with me for the entire day until I finally looked it up.

The mouse was basically Glenn, and by putting him outside my house I was letting go of his drama. Glenn took away my dignity but I was the only one who could stop him from doing it. I felt like a man should be able to go to work and not be degraded by his boss. I had been stuck on how Glenn had wronged me but I realized it wasn't about right or wrong. It was just about my boss abusing his authority and making me feel small. If I didn't let Glenn hurt my feelings I could control my emotions.

The mouse dream was a turning point. Something clicked. I felt Glenn owed me an apology that I was never going to get. I had been fighting for so long thinking that the world owed me something. Certainly after the hell my daughter had gone through the world owed me.

I was always looking for payback. All my thinking had been negative. It was all I knew. I made the decision that day to always be happy for others even if I didn't like them. It was a simple philosophy but it was going to take a lot of practice. It was about gratitude. It was about service. It was about putting others before myself. It dawned on me that the meaning of life was to know yourself; to accept yourself. I had heard it before but it had never meant anything to me. I had always been scared. I had always been running. I was lying to myself. We as humans lie a lot, and then continue to lie to cover up more lies, because we don't know ourselves. We aren't comfortable with who we are. I was finally comfortable with myself. Now I wasn't running. I felt loved by Nicole and Vivien. I felt the love of a family. It was a fulfilled love. I didn't need anything else. I didn't need to look for something to fill the hole. I had an amazing wife who loved me for who I was. She didn't care about my job.

The amount of stress I dealt with had pushed my brain to the limit. The only solution I had was giving up. If I gave up maybe events would take a different course. Sometimes it was better to be lucky then to be right. It just seemed I wasn't getting anywhere with Glenn. If I tried a different tactic I might get a better result. Sometimes the best answer was to retreat. As Sun Tzu said in *The Art of War*, "Appear weak when you are strong, and strong when you are weak."

The next day the attorney called with a deal. If I dropped my lawsuit the Department would promote Glenn and transfer him to another city. I would never see him again. The Department would also add a no-retaliation clause into their harassment training for new employees.

"What's the other option?" I asked.

"The other option is to sue the Department for monetary damages."

"How long will that take?" I asked.

"Two to four years. In the meantime you'll be stuck working under Glenn."

I took the path of least resistance and pulled my lawsuit. Glenn got his promotion and the office threw a party for him. It was office politics. No matter what I said or did they loved him. I was finally left alone which was all I ever wanted.

Chapter Fourteen

THE GAME CHANGER

When Vivien turned seven we looked into brain surgery. If we could find where the seizures were coming from we might be able to take out that bad part of the brain. In order to do this we needed another EEG. Before we could do the EEG we needed to do another MRI and an MRA. The MRA was a Magnetic Resonance Angiography that used a magnetic field, radio frequency waves, and produced images of the major arteries. It was more detailed than the MRI. A liquid dye was injected into Vivien so that they could be certain if the arteries in her brain had any abnormalities.

For the EEG we needed to take Vivien off her medication and wait for her to have a seizure. It was a long and tedious process. We were in the hospital for eight days.

The hospital had said they had a ward just for epilepsy patients, but they lied. It wasn't equipped for an overnight EEG. It wasn't equipped for any kind of epilepsy observation.

We had to share our room with a handful of patients. None of them had epilepsy or seizures. No one could understand why Vivien's head was wrapped in gauze with wires sticking out. No one could understand the smell of burnt glue that lingered in the air.

We tried to make the best of our stay since we couldn't leave our room. Vivien was upset. She cried at first but the more her medication was reduced the more she got lost in her own world. The spark in her eyes dimmed. She became delayed. Vivien wasn't herself when she was off her medication. She was slow. I knew she would need to be on medication for the rest of her life. She couldn't even understand her favorite joke.

"Vivien, how do you count cows?" I asked.

"I don't know," replied Vivien.

"With a cow-culator!"

"I don't get it."

She stared at the wall not making eye contact.

We did what we could to make her stay bearable. Nicole and I had wrapped our heads to make Vivien feel better. I could only stand it for a few minutes and had to take it off. Nicole kept her head wrapped for an entire day. I don't know how Vivien endured eight days with her head wrapped.

I felt like the whole world was against us. I developed a hatred for the hospital staff because no one seemed to care. So many people didn't care. I wanted Vivien to know that I wasn't one of them. I wanted her to know her mother and I were fighting for her. I wanted her to know that I cared.

When I was a child everyone called me a failure. At least that's what I heard. I always felt like a failure. It didn't take much for me to believe this. We were failing at epilepsy but I never let Vivien believe that. I never wanted her to feel like a failure. I never wanted her to think that we didn't have some kind of hope left. She needed to believe she'd be seizure-free someday.

The doctors weren't trying to solve our case like on television. The hospital staff wasn't warm and inviting like I thought they'd be. This wasn't the *Grey's Anatomy* I'd been watching for ten years. They were cold and distant. They went out of their way to make us feel uncomfortable. The hospital was supposed to catch her seizures while she slept. However, nurses came by every hour to take her blood. They weren't supposed to wake her up but they did. They collected the wrong data. There was no communication. If I complained they demanded to know who I was.

"What are you doing here?" A nurse asked with a puzzled look.

"My daughter is here." I replied.

"Visiting hours are over."

"I'm not a visitor. I'm a parent."

"We don't allow parents to be with their children."

"Then who takes care of the other children?" I asked.

She gave me a robotic stare.

"We have wonderful staff here. We can call you when visiting hours are available."

"You're crazy. I'm not leaving my child alone."

"But it's the hospital policy," she insisted.

"It's not my policy. My policy is to stay with my daughter while she goes through this hell."

"If you don't leave I'll have to call security."

"Call the police. I'm not moving."

It was all out war. I wasn't leaving. The hospital staff took out the extra bed so I couldn't use it. They replaced it with a giant crib so I had less space on the floor. I brought in an air mattress, but someone put a hole in the side when I left to get lunch. I bought a green cot for the second night but it disappeared after a day. By the fourth night I was sleeping on the hospital room floor. Nicole slept on a tiny couch that barely fit her body. Things turned stressful. Nicole and I were on edge.

It was like the hospital was trying to break up my family. I finally understood how marriages failed. I finally understood how families fell apart. When things got crazy people left. It was easier to leave. It was harder to stay and work through it. I saw how children were ignored. Loving someone was a sacrifice. You saw people at their lowest in hospitals. Marriage was about putting everyone before yourself. Being a parent was the same. You put your kid before yourself. You loved someone because of his or her flaws. I finally saw that Nicole and I were both broken. I fell in love with this beautiful woman and now we were just trying to hold our lives together.

Dr. S. came by on the fourth day. I had hoped he would be there every day but he wasn't. He didn't seem interested in the EEG reading. He talked about himself the entire time.

"I just got back from India. You should really go. It's

breathtaking."

"We can't travel anywhere until our daughter is seizure free," said Nicole.

"Are you finding any seizures?" I asked.

"No but no news is good news."

"Except when it comes to epilepsy."

"All we can do is wait."

We spent the week waiting for seizures. I looked forward to running errands or getting lunch just to get out of the room. Anything to break away from the boredom of waiting.

We watched movies and made drawings. We danced and made up songs. We taped signs to the window asking for people down below to send up pizza. Strangers waved up to the fifth floor but the pizza never arrived.

Dr. S. cancelled the EEG on the eighth day for insurance reasons. Vivien had a lot of brain activity but no seizures. The hospital wanted the room for someone else and insurance didn't want to pay. We weren't considered high priority.

We packed our things and left defeated.

A month later we met with Dr. S. to go over our week-long EEG at the hospital. It was a breaking point. We were tired of waiting hours to see a man that couldn't fix our daughter.

"There's not much left to do," said Dr. S.

"There has to be something else we can do?" Nicole begged.

"Maybe a new medication," said Dr. S. "I don't think it will work though."

This man I had put all my hopes and dreams into now

appeared to be a real shithead.

We had been seeing him for six years and all he offered was medication. He was nothing but smoke and mirrors, playing on the emotions of scared parents. We had showered him with gifts for years hoping that he might make an extra effort but he never did.

"Why change her medication when it's been working?" I asked. "She hasn't had any seizures in months."

"This new medication is a better medication."

"What about brain surgery?" I asked.

"She isn't a candidate for brain surgery."

"How do you know? You didn't even catch a seizure?"

"You'll be lucky if she doesn't turn out retarded."

"Why would you say that?" I asked.

"It's the truth."

"I don't care if it's the truth. You can't rob us of our hope. It's all we have."

There was no apology. No empathy. Just more medications. I hated him. I wanted to punch him in the throat.

He prescribed a new medication that caused Vivien to have even worse seizures than before. We switched back to the old medication and looked for a new doctor.

Nicole searched the Internet in tears that night. She found a doctor in Los Angeles that specialized in epilepsy at Children's Hospital. It was the hospital we had left but now it was our only shot at beating epilepsy. Children's Hospital had changed staff and created a unit specifically for epilepsy. It looked like a different place now. It looked like a place where we might have some hope.

We met with Dr. Hope who had moved from the east coast to establish the new epilepsy program in Los

Angeles. That wasn't really her name but I thought it was fitting. We liked her immediately because she valued the parents' input. She listened to us. She asked us questions about Vivien that no other doctor had ever bothered to ask. She looked over Vivien's brain scans and was able to explain them to Nicole and me in simple terms. Dr. Shithead always spoke in medical terms that I never understood. When Dr. Hope spoke everything made sense. It took Dr. Hope twenty minutes to explain something that no other doctor could for the past six years.

"It isn't the one spot on Vivien's brain that is causing seizures. It's most likely the entire side because her brain didn't fully develop."

Dr. Hope pointed to Vivien's MRI. She pointed to a different area of the brain. An area that Dr. Shithead never mentioned. The new area looked badly deformed. There was a large dark mass. Vivien's brain had not fully developed because of her fetal stroke. She was lucky to be alive.

"I can also see by blood tests that Nicole has a genetic blood clotting disorder. If you had known that, some blood thinners during pregnancy might have changed things."

"This is completely different than what we've been told by the last doctor," I said.

"I'm afraid he was giving you bad advice."

"Unbelievable."

"Brain surgery isn't out of the question," said Dr. Hope. "We just have to pin point where the seizures are coming from in her brain. Unfortunately, we can't use any of the data from the last EEG so we have to do another one."

A month later we were back in the hospital for another EEG. Vivien was disappointed but now she knew what to expect. I showered her with gifts hoping it would ease her pain. She loved American Girl dolls so I bought her one every day that we were at the hospital. I spoiled her because I felt so guilty. She had such bad memory loss I was afraid she would forget her childhood. She never complained. She never said she couldn't handle the hospital. She had amazing courage.

I also showered the hospital staff with gifts. I learned the second time around that you had to be nice to them or they turned on you. I had to humble myself and lower my expectations and then lower them some more. I brought them gifts so they would remember us and put a name to our faces. Every day I went down the block to the bakery and brought back the most unusual cake I could find.

"Did you see that cake made out of Twix bars that the Knox family brought us?!"

The hospital was ready for Vivien when we arrived. This hospital wanted us there. They wanted to cure Vivien of her epilepsy. They wrapped her head in gauze and hooked her up to an IV. There was a video monitoring room across from Vivien's room, recording all of her movements. Dr. Hope was on call twenty-four hours and gave strict orders not to disturb Vivien while she slept. She checked on us daily. Vivien's medication was slowly lowered and she once again became slow and delayed. We fell back into the old routine of trying to kill time. Watching movies, playing dress up with Vivien's dolls, drawing pictures, and dreaming of a life without seizures.

On the seventh day Vivien had a big hairy seizure at six in the morning. Everything was working correctly and Dr. Hope was able to capture it on video. It was so bad that

Vivien needed three doses of Ativan to stop the seizure.

After seeing the controlled seizure I thought that all was lost. Dr. Hope hadn't been excited about this seizure. Nothing looked promising. The seizure had been all over her brain. As far as I could see it was coming from four different places. There was no way any surgeon could do brain surgery in four different places.

Dr. Hope brought Nicole and I into a small room across from Vivien's room. She closed the door and I waited for the bad news. My mind was in a fog. Dr. Hope was speaking but I couldn't make out her words. She pulled a small device the size of a silver dollar from her lab coat pocket. There was a wire connected to it. She smiled and handed it to me.

"I think Vivien would be perfect for the VNS," said Dr. Hope.

"What's VNS?" I asked.

"It stands for Vagus Nerve Stimulator. It's a medical device that delivers electrical impulses to the vagus nerve."

It was just the hope we needed. After all the doctors we had been through who were pushing medications, this one doctor was finally giving us hope. We had gone through so many doctors and not one of them had ever mentioned VNS. I was angry but I trusted our new doctor. I didn't understand medicine but I understood movies. In every movie there is a person that needs to overcome the odds. We needed to beat epilepsy. Then there is the person that appears when all seems lost. This person shows the way out. Dr. Hope changed the course of our lives and let us believe we could win. She was that person in the movie that points the main character in the right direction when he or she is about to give up. I felt born again. We just might beat epilepsy.

The Vagus Nerve Stimulator had been around for more than twenty years and I was annoyed this was the first time we were discussing it.

"It's like a pacemaker for your brain," Dr. Hope said. "A small generator can be programmed by a physician to stimulate the vagus nerve in the neck."

"This is amazing," I said.

"So, if two or more medications failed then VNS can be approved for patients. You're already approved and insurance will cover everything."

The technology was beyond me. I couldn't see how something so small could stop seizures. The success rate was more than 80%. I liked the odds considering I had graduated college with a 70% average. Vivien would be the eighth child to receive VNS on the west coast.

Some VNS patients had an increase in seizures while others saw no change at all. The side effects seemed minor. They could be cough, sore throat, hoarseness, upset stomach, nausea and headache. The device needed to be implanted on the left side of the chest near the heart. Another incision needed to be made in the throat to guide the wire to the vagus nerve. This would require Vivien to have surgery. I didn't want Vivien to have surgery but I wanted her to be seizure-free. It was a much easier procedure than brain surgery. I was just skeptical because everything else had failed.

Nicole wanted to get it done as soon as possible. I needed more time to think. I didn't want to put Vivien through any more hospital stays. I felt like she had gone through enough and needed a few years off.

A series of events quickly changed my mind. Vivien's seizures were getting worse. The seizures had a pattern but the pattern was changing. Vivien was staying awake four nights a week with insomnia. We would put her to bed and then she wouldn't be able to sleep. She might fall asleep for an hour and wake up unable to go back to sleep. Her mind was racing. She was overwhelmed with anxiety and depression.

Our lives were spiraling out of control. We were running out of time trying to find an answer. The lack of sleep was the hardest. It interfered with our work day. People at work didn't think I was losing sleep over a sick child. They just assumed I was hung over. It didn't matter how many times I told them about my daughter's epilepsy. I always got the same comment at work.

"Rough night?" asked a coworker. "Maybe you should ease up on the partying."

I slept most of the time at my office or in my car. Vivien was going to school but she was not able to concentrate on her schoolwork. She was failing. Even though she was in a new school that catered to her special needs she was way behind. The school was great but they didn't fully understand the depth of her illness. The school didn't understand why she couldn't sleep. They thought it was as easy as closing her eyes. The lack of sleep was causing her stress and in return causing her to have seizures. Her seizures were getting stronger. They had taken on a mind of their own. I finally understood why ancient tribes thought people with seizures were possessed. During a few seizures Vivien would talk slowly and in a deep voice.

She would insist that we let her go back to sleep.

"I'm just tired. Let me go back to sleep," she growled.

"I think you're having a seizure," I said.

"No, I'm fine. Let me sleep."

The seizure was lying to us, trying to overtake my daughter's mind and kill her. If I let her go back to sleep during a seizure she would die.

After dropping Vivien off at school one morning, I was halfway home when I saw a truck drive through a red light at an intersection. I could see that the driver was having a seizure. Somehow he made it through the intersection without crashing. His truck came to a rolling stop into the front bumper of another car going in the opposite direction.

I made a u-turn and raced to help him. When I got there a motorcycle cop was getting off his bike and approaching the man. The cop opened the truck door and pulled the man by his arm while he was still having a seizure. I jumped out of my car and ran to the officer.

"Don't move him," I yelled. "He's having a seizure!"

"He looks drunk!" the cop scoffed.

The cop tugged on the man's shirt but he was wearing his seatbelt.

"No, it's a seizure."

"How do you know?" the cop asked.

"My daughter has epilepsy. Just leave him alone."

"Shouldn't we pin him to the ground?" the cop asked.

"No, he's wearing his seat belt. He's safe. Just wait for the paramedics."

"What if he swallows his tongue?"

"He won't. You can't swallow your tongue during a

seizure."

The cop pushed him back inside the truck. The man was having a partial focal seizure. His eyes were fluttering. His arms and head were shaking. I called 911 while the cop held him. Traffic backed up. More police arrived to direct traffic. The paramedics arrived and I directed them to the man.

"He's having a partial focal seizure," I explained.

"How do you know that?" Now the paramedic scoffed at me.

"My daughter has seizures."

"Are you sure he's not intoxicated?"

"I'm sure it's a seizure."

"Just back off," said the paramedic. "Let the professionals hand this."

No one believed the man was having a seizure. They all seemed to think he was drunk and had caused a traffic accident.

The paramedics didn't give him any rescue medication. If they had rescue medication they could have stopped the seizure. They carried Narcon for heroin overdoses but nothing for seizures. They loaded him on a gurney and drove off.

I thought of Vivien and what might happen to her when she was older. She could have a seizure walking across the street and collapse in traffic. Who would be there to help her? Would any of these "professionals" know what a seizure was or would they just assume she was drunk?

A strange feeling swept over me. Something felt wrong with Vivien. There were days that I didn't argue with myself and checked on her just in case. Most times I was wrong, and thought I was being an overly protective father. I drove back to her school just in case. Vivien's class was on a break. Children were playing on the playground. Vivien was sitting on a bench by herself. I hurried over to her. I hugged her but she didn't hug me back. She seemed confused.

"Are you okay?" I asked.

"I don't have any friends, Daddy," she mumbled.

"You have to make friends."

"No. My teacher said if I sit on the 'buddy bench' then kids will come over and want to make friends with me."

The "buddy bench" broke my heart. It was just a bench but Vivien believed it was something special. It didn't work for Vivien. She didn't understand it. She didn't know that life was cruel sometimes. The truth was she didn't have any friends because others didn't understand her epilepsy. Family and friends didn't want their kids to play with her because they thought her epilepsy was contagious or that their children would be traumatized. Time and space were a problem. Her mobility was off. Sometimes when I left for work Vivien thought I was leaving her alone. She didn't connect that her mother was in the other room. I kept hoping she was going to get better but I was lying to myself. The school didn't understand her needs either. They had her trapped in the special needs category. The school wasn't trying to help her get out of that label. She was parked in one place and no one had any expectations for her to succeed. She was all alone.

I was concerned on so many levels. As a stand-up comedian I was worried that Vivien wouldn't understand humor because of her seizures. I felt selfish for thinking that, but it was important to me. It was something only other comedians would understand. I wanted her to have the gift of humor. I wanted her to understand sarcasm, but I knew she wasn't there yet.

It was hard for her to adjust to conformity. She was easy-going. She was sweet and kind. She was such a good kid. She never complained or talked back or rolled her eyes or questioned me as a parent. She was the complete opposite of every other kid I knew. She didn't understand schoolyard politics. She didn't understand adult things. She still believed in Santa Claus and the tooth fairy and I wanted to keep it that way. She just wanted to be a kid but her epilepsy had made her sad, empty, and lost at school.

"We can fix this," I said. "I'll talk to Mrs. Benson."

"Who's Mrs. Benson?" Vivien asked.

"She's your third grade teacher. Don't you remember?"

"No, I don't know where I am."

"We're at your school."

She looked up at me. A spark of recognition filled her eyes. She knew who I was but she was delayed. It was frightening because she was deteriorating right in front of me. It might have been her medicine. It might have been the heat. It might have just been an off-day but she wasn't herself. She threw her arms around me and cried. I was scared that my daughter was losing her mind. We cried together on the buddy bench. I picked her up and realized for the first time that she was getting bigger. At some point she would be too big to carry or lift. I carried her to my car and we drove home.

Later that day, I had to be at the office and Nicole had a teacher's conference at Vivien's school. Vivien seemed fine. We were going over Vivien's seizure care plan with the school. Nicole got a babysitter for Vivien. It was one of the few times we left her alone but my mother was on vacation and we were out of options. I never knew how anyone was able to juggle a family and work. Nicole was only going to be gone for an hour and the babysitter was a trusted friend we had known for years.

Judy was a nurse so I figured we were covered under any medical emergency. I fully trusted Judy and I had no doubt she would know what to do if anything happened.

Nicole left the house and Vivien had a seizure twenty minutes later. Judy called me and said that Vivien had thrown up. Every time my phone rang it was bad news. It was always another seizure. I dreaded answering the phone. Judy couldn't get a hold of Nicole. I could hear Vivien screaming in the background. It was out of the ordinary that Vivien would have a seizure in the late afternoon but the vomiting was always a good indication that she was going to have a seizure. She had also seemed off earlier in the day.

"Something's wrong with Vivien," groaned Judy.

"I'm having a seizure!" Vivien screamed.

"You've got to give her the rescue medication, Judy," I insisted. "It's on the top shelf in the closet."

"No, she's fine," insisted Judy.

"She's not fine!"

"But she's talking and standing up."

"She could still be having a seizure."

"Help me Daddy!" Vivien screamed.

I was helpless.

"Judy I need you to give her that shot now!" I yelled.

"I can't. I've never given anyone a shot before."

"I thought you were a nurse?"

"I am but I can't do this!"

Judy, the nurse, was frozen in fear. When it came down to it there were few people that were up to the fight. I called 911. I gave the operator my address and told them that Vivien had epilepsy. I called Nicole but she didn't answer. I knew her phone was sitting in her purse because she was in a meeting with Vivien's teachers. I raced home but I was a half hour away. Traffic in Los Angeles was beginning to back up. I called Judy and was relieved to hear a fireman answer the phone. The emergency operator had come through. The fire department was only a few minutes from our home. They knew us well. I owed my life to all those first responders.

"She's okay now," said a fireman. "I gave her the rescue medication and her seizure stopped right away. She has a temperature of 101 degrees so I would watch her closely."

"I will. Thank you so much," I said.

I got home and held Vivien. Every time she had a seizure I held her a little tighter. I watched her a little longer and tried to live in the moment. She seemed okay but I took her to the hospital just in case and had her checked out.

On the way home I stopped at the pharmacy to get some liquid Motrin for Vivien. She had a headache and the Motrin always helped. I took the bottle up to the counter. The pharmacy was alive with the buzz that the Lakers had just won. Several people had come inside wearing Lakers jerseys, cheering to other customers buying beer. The woman behind the counter was ecstatic.

"Did you watch the game? She asked.

"No."

"Well, why not? Everyone else has. Have you been living in a cave?"

"I've been in the hospital."

"Well, you should have seen it."

I was in such a daze I didn't even know what day it was. I was so focused on Vivien's epilepsy that I didn't even know what was going on in society. I hadn't seen a game in years. Epilepsy had held us hostage for so long that I was used to the seclusion. I wasn't doing a very good job at taking care of myself. Epilepsy had changed the dynamics of our family and taken a toll on our souls. I didn't realize we were living like hermits away from society. I just wanted our old life back.

I knew at that moment we were going to get the VNS. I needed someone to be with Vivien 24/7 watching over her, someone who wouldn't fold under pressure. I needed to join society again just as much as Vivien did. We needed to get back on track. We needed VNS Therapy.

I needed something to put my faith in, like VNS Therapy. I had stopped praying because it didn't seem to be doing anything. I had spent so many years in Catholic school. I had spent thousands of hours praying and going to church, mass, church groups, after school programs. I thought someone owed me something. Wasn't that the whole point? Wasn't that the way it worked? I put in the effort and I was supposed to get back tenfold. Why wasn't it working? Everyone had given me a promise that if I just followed this certain path everything would turn out right. The only problem was that everything had turned to shit.

Everything had gone off course and was spiraling out of control. I didn't have any faith left so I turned to science. The VNS made sense.

I didn't know how to tell an eight-year-old she had to have surgery. The date was set for the month of August. We only had a month to prepare. We couldn't surprise her. We had made the mistake of not telling her she was getting the flu shot when she was younger. We wanted to be honest with her. We couldn't wait until the day before and surprise her. She wanted to be told of any crisis so she could prepare for it on her own terms.

I happened to watch the movie *Iron Man* that night, about a man that suffers a chest injury and builds a suit to protect himself. It would be the perfect sell if Vivien was a boy. I needed the Bionic Woman. I ordered the DVDs online and Vivien really loved them. It was a series about Jamie Sommers, who almost dies in a sky diving accident. She is rebuilt with bionics to be stronger and faster. Vivien was going to be stronger and faster. She had the courage and determination to change her life for the better.

Before we could get the VNS surgery Vivien needed to take a sleep study. During her last EEG she had had breathing problems and Dr. Hope wasn't sure if she could be put under. Her heart rate had sky-rocketed to over 170 beats per minute. Her breathing was so rapid and her oxygen level was so low everyone was concerned. A dozen medical professionals stood over Vivien for hours trying to figure out what was wrong with her breathing.

The sleep study was in a half-empty office building fifteen minutes from our home. We arrived in the evening and checked into an office that had been converted into two bedrooms. Vivien was hooked up with more wires than she had during her two EEG visits. She had one that was clamped to her nose and I wondered how she was going to sleep.

There was only one man running the night shift. He reminded me of Lurch from *The Addams Family*. It was one of Vivien's favorite shows so he didn't bother her. I wasn't sure if we were going to make it out of there alive. He insisted that we leave Vivien by herself and come back in the morning.

"Not going to happen," I said.

"Suit yourself but there's no place for the parents to sleep."

There was a queen size bed and a lazy boy chair in our room. The room smelled musky, like an old crime scene that had been scrubbed down. Nicole slept in a leather La-Z-Boy chair. I lay down next to Vivien, hoping somehow to make sure she didn't have a seziure. It was torture but she fell asleep quickly. I managed to stay awake until the sun came up. We packed our stuff and went home exhausted.

The next day Vivien was covered in red marks. She had hundreds of bed bug bites. Half of my body was also bitten, but just one side because I didn't sleep under the covers like Vivien. I had lain on my side so my bed bug attack wasn't as bad. I did have one bite between my eyes that stayed with me for a year.

We tossed everything in bags and put them in the garage. We fumigated the house and hired a beagle named Bailey to sniff through everything. Somehow we didn't take any bed bugs home with us. The sleep study number was disconnected when I tried to complain. The good news was that the sleep study data was sent to Children's Hospital and Vivien was able to have her VNS Therapy procedure.

We arrived at Children's Hospital early on the day of the surgery. We had a few hours before the procedure. There was a playground in the front of the hospital. I was glad they had a place for kids to play. It was a good diversion. Nicole and Vivien ran around the playground. I tried to act like everything was okay but I was dying inside. A heavy depression had set in that I hadn't felt in years. I had never wanted a drink more badly than at that moment. I just wanted something to numb the pain.

I realized I hadn't had a drink in six years. Not because I had a problem but because my priorities had changed. I needed to be sober in case something happened to Vivien. I knew I had to hold it together for my family. Giving up was easy. Anyone could do it. The hardest part was keeping it together while the world crumbled around me.

We checked into the front desk an hour later. I always filled out the hospital paperwork because of Nicole's hearing. It was hard for her to hear people and I tried to make our hospital stays easier. The women behind the admissions counter gave me a clipboard with forms to fill out. My hand was trembling. I couldn't think.

"What's your daughter's birthday?" she asked.

"I don't know. Sorry but I'm drawing a blank."

"What's your address?"

"I'm not sure."

I felt like an idiot. The woman took mercy on me and took the clipboard from me. She set it down on the counter.

"We can fill this out later," she said.

"Thank you."

A girl escorted us to a surgery waiting room and dressed Vivien in faded tiger pajamas. They looked like they had been worn a million times. A nurse took her vital signs. She struggled to get the IV in her arm. Vivien moaned in pain.

"It's okay, baby," I said. "Be strong."

"I'm trying, Daddy," she whispered.

"It's going to be okay. I promise."

I wanted to be her hero but at that moment it was too painful. She saw the tears in my eyes and gave me a hug.

"I don't tell you that I'm scared because I don't want you to be scared, Daddy."

"It's okay to be scared. Real courage is being scared."

"I'm trying to be brave."

She always seemed to say the right things to me in my time of need. Nicole held Vivien's hand.

"We're at the top of that mountain I was telling you about," said Nicole. "You're almost over the mountain and we will be all done. I love you."

"I love you too, Mommy."

Another nurse gave Vivien a grape drink to calm her down. It kicked in ten minutes later. She arched her back and looked up at the ceiling.

"Can we change my middle name to Donkey?" She giggled. Then she fell asleep. It was nice not to see her in pain. They wheeled her out of the room past the other children waiting to have operations, then down a hall where a nurse stopped us.

"Sorry but you can't go any further. Hospital staff only. She'll be okay."

I tried to believe her. Nicole and I watched her wheel

Vivien down a long hallway and then disappear behind another set of doors. It felt like we had never left Vivien alone but I knew that wasn't true.

We went downstairs to the chapel. Nicole wanted to pray so I waited in the hallway. I watched parents and children roam the hallways like zombies. They were drained from trying to get from one doctor appointment to the next. We shared that in common. We had the same look, like only prison inmates could recognize. We were confused and exhausted. We hated being there but we didn't have a choice. I was one of the lucky ones that day because, in a way, we were getting paroled. We got to go home while the others had to stay. A woman holding a baby approached me.

"Is the chapel closed?" she asked.

"No, my wife is in there."

"Aren't you going inside?"

"No, I can't bring myself to pray anymore. I just can't believe in a higher power when I live in Los Angeles."

"I'm the opposite. I think my faith has increased. I've seen you around the hospital. How's your daughter?"

"She's upstairs getting surgery for her epilepsy."

Her baby couldn't have been more than six months old. His skin was a dark orange color and he had a tube taped to his nose.

"How's your baby?" I asked.

"He needs a liver transplant but we don't have a donor."

"I'm sorry."

"It's not fair. Life isn't fair."

"I wish I could fix this."

"I know. You die a little each day but you wake up and

make the best of it anyways."

I felt guilty that we were going home and she was staying and there was nothing I could do about it. So, I did what I did best and cried with a mother and her baby in the hallway of Children's Hospital.

The VNS Therapy procedure was over in an hour and Nicole and I went back upstairs to the recovery room. Vivien woke up a half hour later and a nurse gave her a grape popsicle.

Two hours later we were able to go home. I pulled the car around and Nicole helped Vivien into the car. We drove home in silence hoping we had made the right decision with the VNS Therapy.

By the next day Vivien was dancing around the house and eating a McDonald's Happy Meal. I was surprised at how quickly she bounced back. She was back in school the next week and her scars started to heal nicely. Two weeks later the VNS was turned on and placed on the lowest setting.

The only major side effect she had was a change in her voice sometimes, which she called her "fan voice." It sounded like she was talking into a fan. When it went away she missed it. I had gone into the surgery hoping to go one month seizure-free, so when we hit the two-month mark it was all worth it. We had two months of seizure freedom that turned into six months.

We completed our first epilepsy walk around the Rose Bowl in Pasadena. Vivien was so excited that she was seizure-free. I was cautious that this machine in my child's chest would work but even I believed that she was cured.

Then one morning Vivien sat up in bed and gasped for

air.

"I'm having a seizure Daddy!" she screamed.

I grabbed the VNS magnet and swiped it across her heart several times. The seizure stopped and Vivien quickly fell back asleep. I was devastated that Vivien wasn't cured. Six months were down the drain and we had to start over. Then it dawned on me that the VNS had worked. It had done its job and stopped the seizure when I swiped the magnet.

In the following months Vivien had several more seizures but they seemed smaller. She was able to recover quickly and go back to sleep. Instead of being negative I looked at the VNS like it was a positive. It was another tool in our toolbox that was helping Vivien, along with her medication.

After the VNS Therapy all of the seizures were controllable. We could also swipe the magnet if we thought Vivien was going to have a seizure, just to be on the safe side. The more the VNS went off the better it was for her brain in a sense. The VNS was always correcting her brain. Vivien was able to speak and say what was wrong. She was able to bounce back, whereas before it would take her a week to recover. I felt better about carrying the magnet in my pocket than a syringe full of a rescue medication. Nicole and I kept magnets in our cars and put one in Vivien's backpack. All of Vivien's teachers carried them around at school just in case of an emergency. I felt better knowing that Vivien had something watching her twenty-four hours a day.

Little by little her life changed. The months went by and the seizures stopped. There were still bad days but it was a far cry from the years of being hunted down by seizures. The puzzle pieces of her life were coming back together. I started to notice things that I'd forgotten; things that most of us just take for granted. Vivien didn't need help brushing her teeth or putting on her clothes in the morning. Her mood was better. Her anxiety and depression were gone. She wasn't as tired as she normally was. She had more energy. Her mind wasn't foggy. She wasn't mumbling to herself throughout the day. She slept through the night. Her insomnia disappeared.

She wasn't afraid to go to school anymore. She had a sense of security. She no longer worried about her seizures. The seizure monster wasn't chasing her anymore. She had the gift of time on her side. She wanted to venture out and see the world. Her vision, speech, balance, hearing, and language were improving. She was starting to be the little girl she deserved to be. She had fought so hard for a better life and the VNS was rewarding her for it.

Her teachers said she was a joy in their classrooms. She was excelling at reading and writing. No more tears over math problems because everything clicked. There were no more trips to the hospital in the middle of the night. No more missed days of school and having to appear in front of the school board to explain ourselves. It was funny that when she stopped getting hit by lightning her memory improved.

When Vivien's seizures got better I promised myself I would do all the things I had put aside. I started writing again and doing stand-up comedy. I went through boxes in the garage and downsized on material items. I lost twenty-five pounds. Then I gained it back. I had a tattoo removed and I found my biological mom.

My adoption had always been a major issue in my life. I had always felt a sense of rejection due to being adopted. I felt alone. I had even gone to a psychic ten years before in Pasadena. She had said that my biological mother didn't want to be found. I always carried that in the back of my mind.

My sister had found her biological parents when she was eighteen. She had been the product of a one-night stand and they were no longer together. My sister's adoption was open so she had all their information available when she turned eighteen. My sister was forbidden to tell me for ten years about her biological mother. My mother was convinced I'd commit suicide if I found out. That was the sad part about my family, we had so many secrets.

I met my sister's biological mother one time. She was a sweet woman but had her problems. The guilt of giving up her baby for adoption had consumed her and she could never get past it.

A year later I met my sister's biological father. Before Nicole and I got married I rented a room in my sister's home. There was a knock on my door at six in the morning. I slept late in those days so I was angry that someone was knocking on my bedroom door so early. When I opened the door a strange man was standing there.

"Do you know where the hand ball courts are?" he asked.

It was such a bizarre question, and one that my sister would have asked. My sister was one of those people who thought everyone thought the same way she did. She hadn't said anything about having her biological father come to visit. Normally, I would have been scared that someone had broken into my house but I knew who he was immediately.

He looked just like my sister but in the body of a fifty year old man. He was also partially covered in blood because he had run over an animal on the way to the airport. Then he tried to carry the animal on the plane but security stopped him. He didn't bother to change his clothes, knowing my sister was going to pick him up at the airport.

I was blown away by the DNA footprint. My sister was just like her biological father, whom she hadn't seen in twenty years. Before this I had always thought we were created out of our social surroundings. Now I was certain it was a combination of biology and social circumstances. Her bio dad stayed for a week until they couldn't stand each other. They were both stubborn and always right. One morning he took off and we never heard from him again.

I hired a private investigator, who took less than a week to find my biological mother. I felt guilty I had waited so long. I would never have found her on my own. The private investigator found my birth records that had been transferred by hand to an outdated system in 1990. The county destroyed all adoption information after ten years. I had tried several times over the years to find my bio mom but my adoption was closed. The County of Los Angeles did a great job of not helping anyone who was adopted find his or her biological family.

My birth mother was living in Nevada. She had twice lived within ten miles of me. The private investigator sent me a picture with her three adult sons. I didn't look like my half brothers but I could see myself in her. She reminded me of the actress Sarah Poulsen. We had the same eyes. Her smile was just like mine when she tilted her head back. We had the same jaw line. I had never seen another adult that looked like me. Until Vivien I had never been able to stare into a photo and feel a connection.

My emotions exploded in every direction. Everything was happening so fast I wasn't sure I could process all the information. I had waited my entire life for this moment. I didn't know what to do with the information.

"What's her address?" I asked.

"I'll send it to you but I have to warn you that I don't think she wants to be found."

"Why?" I asked.

"I've been doing this for 25 years and I know when a person doesn't want to be found. She's moved around a lot and she's not on social media. I got her photos from other relatives. I also spoke to the oldest son in Florida. She had him a year after you were born. I gave him your number. Just be prepared if no one calls you."

"I understand."

"Look on the bright side. You're not inbred. At least you know now that your birth wasn't some kind of disaster. It was probably a one-night stand and she just didn't want to be reminded of the guy she slept with."

"I get it."

I sunk back into my office chair. He was right. No one called me. She was running just like me. My biological mother who had given me up for adoption was in a way a lot like me. Even after being married to the same guy for forty years and having three more sons she didn't want to open old wounds. I couldn't blame her. I had only wanted to find out if she was alive. If she was safe. If she was happy. If she had turned out all right. Sometimes the things we search for so hard, to fill the holes in life, leave us even more empty inside. I embraced the loneliness again.

I was hurt, but as the days went by I felt less and less broken. I appreciated my own mother more. She might have adopted me but she was my real mother. She was the only mother I knew. She cared about me. This was the last hole in my life that needed to be filed. All the panic attacks and all the therapy finally made sense. I was finally enough.

The mother who took me home three days after I was born. The mother who fed me rice cereal and changed my diapers. The mother who sang to me as a child. The mother who prayed every night that I would live. The mother who made my lunch and wrote little notes that she loved me. The mother who drove me to school. Who took care of me when I was sick with asthma. The mother who drove me to countless doctor trips. The mother who showed up to care for my daughter who was suffering with epilepsy. My mother who was always there for me. I loved my mother. My birth mom I never knew.

A year after the VNS Therapy procedure Vivien woke up early and got dressed. She made herself some waffles and put together a Lego Barbie house. She was no longer quiet and sad on the drive to school.

"Daddy, what does a cow use for math?"

"I don't know?"

"A cow-culator!"

We both laughed but for different reasons. She thought the joke was funny. I laughed because she got it. The spark was back in her eyes. It was a deep wonderful happiness that I had long forgotten. Before the VNS she didn't have any interests. She was just going through each day waiting for another seizure. She was moving through life with purpose now. She was grounded.

"I feel good today," said Vivien.

"I'm glad."

"I mean it. I've felt so lost for such a long time. Today is going to be a good day."

She was growing up and I was okay with it. It was the first serious conversation we had ever had. It was short but powerful. She was acknowledging all of her problems in the past due to epilepsy.

"I guess it's true what they say about the rain," said Vivien.

"What's that?" I asked.

"Sometimes there's a rainbow at the end."

"So true," I smiled.

That old warm fuzzy feeling crept into my bones. I felt safe. I felt there was really going to be a future for my child. Everything was going to be okay. The VNS wasn't a cure and Vivien was still taking seizure medication. However, we didn't have to add another medication with the VNS or strengthen the one she had. Beyond the seizures the VNS was helping her mature. Our lives had fallen back into place. We had our child back and I wasn't going to blink.

I walked Vivien to her class but this time she let go of my hand and disappeared into a crowd of her friends on the schoolyard. A group of girls surrounded Vivien and gave her hugs. It was amazing to see her interact at school instead of cry. I turned to leave thinking this would be the last day Vivien would want me to walk her to class. I remembered being embarrassed of my parents at her age. I was so thankful she had her friends that cared about her at school. I didn't mind stepping down and being the embarrassing parent. This was the turning point in our lives. She called after me from her circle of friends.

"Bye Daddy. I love you."

I waved and melted in the warmth of the morning sun.

ABOUT THE AUTHOR

Mike Knox is a writer and stand-up comedian who has performed at The Comedy Store, the Hollywood Improv, and the Pasadena Ice House. A former corrections officer at California State Prison, Los Angeles County, he is currently employed as a parole agent by the California department of corrections and rehabilitation. He lives in Valencia, California, with his wife and daughter; for the gift of their love, he feels both lucky and unworthy.

ABOUT THE PUBLISHER

The Sager Group was founded in 1984. In 2012 it was chartered as a multi-media artists' and writers' consortium, with the intent of empowering those who make art—an umbrella beneath which makers can pursue, and profit from, their craft directly, without gatekeepers. TSG publishes eBooks and paper books; manages musical acts and produces live shows; ministers to artists and provides modest grants; and produces documentary, feature, and web-based films. By harnessing the means of production, The Sager Group helps artists help themselves. For more information, please visit www.TheSagerGroup.Net.

Made in the USA
Middletown, DE
19 August 2020